GUNS N' ROSES

GUNS N' ROSES

THE WORLD'S MOST OUTRAGEOUS HARD ROCK BAND

PAUL ELLIOTT

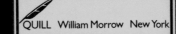

QUILL William Morrow New York

Acknowledgement: some source material has previously appeared in Sounds,
Kerrang!, RIP, RAW, Rolling Stone and Music Connection –
Paul Elliott.

Acknowledgments

The publishers would like to thank the following
organisations and individuals for their kind permission
to reproduce the photographs in this book:

All photographs by Ian Tilton except for the following:

Greg Freeman 10,11,17,18,19 1,30,31 t.1,31 b.1,31 b.r,32 t,
32 b.1,46 t.r,46 b.r,80

Tim Jarvis 36 t.r,36 b.1,36 b.r,37 b.1,37 t.1,37 t.r,37 b.r

L.F.I/Lynn McAfee 13,/Ilpo Musto 36 t.1,/Sam Hain 44–45

Pictorial Press/J. Mayer 8,/Bob Lease 12

Relay Photos 24,28,34 b,66 b,73,75,76/Justin Thomas 9,34 t,
41 t.1,44 1,58 main,70–71/Jon Conrad 16/Jodi Summers
26–27,72 b,/Alex Solca 41 b.r,/Gene Ambo 56,/David
Wainwright 62 b.1,65 main,/Paul Natkin 2–3,72,77

Retna Pictures Ltd./Larry Busacca 25,32 b.r,46 t.l,/
Eddie Malluk 28 b,58 b.r,68 main/Jennifer Rose 57 main,/
Y.Moto 61 main/Tony Mottram 63

Rex Features Ltd., 33,35,45

Recognizing the importance of preserving what has been written, it is
the policy of William Morrow and Company, Inc., and its imprints and
affiliates to have the books it publishes printed on acid-free paper,
and we exert our best efforts to that end.

Library of Congress Card Catalog Number: 90-61077

ISBN 0-688-10054-6

Printed in Great Britain

First U.S. Edition

1 2 3 4 5 6 7 8 9 10

CONTENTS

INTRODUCTION

Guns N' Roses are one of the biggest-selling rock 'n' roll bands on the planet these days, but they're still the same street trash they always were.

Steven's still crazy, Duff's still cool, Izzy's still fazed, Slash is still drunk, Axl's still one bad mother. They're still wild, still louder than hell, still the meanest, rawest rock band in America.

No amount of royalty money could ever make Guns N' Roses clean. Their music will always carry the stink of gasoline alley.

Guns came out of Hollywood in 1987, sweating decadence. Each had ghosted into Los Angeles from Nowhere, USA. Rock 'n' roll is their salvation, their life. They live it hard and fast.

What you're holding is a fly-on-the-wall life history of the most sensational and controversial rock 'n' roll band since the Sex Pistols. Their story ain't pretty. It is rock 'n' roll Babylon personified.

Sex, drugs, violence, here is the shocking truth, from the band's own lips. Follow Guns N' Roses from The Whiskey A Go Go in Los Angeles to the Marquee in London; from Manchester to Dallas and back to Donington from sticky-walled whiskey holes to cowshed coliseums. Taste the reckless life of the road; the sweat, the triumphs, the heartbreak, the excess.

See Guns grow from Hollywood

Paul Elliott.

This band bleeds for its music like no other. Guns N' Roses are the ultimate rock outlaws.

brats into the people's rock 'n' roll band of the late '80s and '90s.

Guns N' Roses are misfits who've caught the mood of the world's restless, estranged youth. Kids picking up guitars want to spit in society's face like Guns N' Roses do.

Here is an eye witness account of the birth of a rock 'n' roll legend.

RAISING HELL IN THE CITY OF ANGELS

The Whiskey A Go Go, Hollywood, Los Angeles, California. 16 March 1987.

Five punks, all rag and bone and psyched stares, spill on to a stage the size of a beer crate. The air is dry and charged, the joint heaving. The guest list would stretch halfway down Sunset Boulevard but few have come just to hang out and drain the bar. Rubber and leather groans as toes arch and necks strain for a clear sight of LA's newest kings of the gutter.

"Guns," bawls a roadie compère, "'N' Fuckin' Roses!!"

The intro tape is 'What's That Noise?' by SOD (Stormtroopers of Death). As it spits and misfires its 57 seconds of hardcore chaos, guitar hands claw up, knuckles whiten. The tape cuts, drummer Steven Adler beats a frenzied cue and the guitars come down hard. They gun 'Reckless Life', hot metal and methedrine.

The lip of the stage is suddenly a blur of headstocks and dripping hair. Limbs thrash and sweat rains. The music kicks and screams.

Steven's blond mane is soon dark with fluid. Shirtless, he works a streamlined kit, quick hands whipping hard. He smiles, alone.

W. Axl Rose, shadowed by Izzy Stradlin' (_left_); Duff McKagan (_right_). Beer drinkers and hell raisers. Vagabonds of the western world.

Axl, tattooed
beat messiah,
on stage at The
Whiskey A Go Go,
Hollywood, USA.

Duff McKagan greases the rhythm with a bass tugged from down around his boots. Tall, lean, Duff moves with a slow sway that's half lazy, half boozy. Under straggles of dirty gold and black, his seems the coolest head in Guns N' Roses.

As scruffy and heavy-lidded as the average big-city wino, Izzy Stradlin' prowls the shadows. He hugs the backline, throttling a big white Gibson and sucking on a chain of cigarettes which he chews into spent ash in seconds. When the riffs turn nasty – stinging like the Sex Pistols on 'It's So Easy' – Izzy's lips curl, teeth clench, his expression sour and intense.

Stage right is Slash, looking like the Ramone that time forgot. Booze brudder. Stripped to the waist. Dark ringlets in his eyes. Head bowed and reeling with the stink of whiskey.

He opens his shoulders and lets his head roll back; seemingly frazzled beyond help, yet his coal-black Les Paul lashes with a tongue like a razor, leads bleeding rage, danger, melancholy.

Alongside coppertan Slash, W Axl Rose seems pale, spectral. He wears just supple purple leather pants sunk into tatty cowboy boots. China-white skin stretches across his rib-cage and appears thin, almost to the point of translucence.

As 'Welcome To The Jungle' coils and rumbles, Axl melts into the shape of the crucifix hung about his neck. His sinewy arms spread, knotted with veins and blue with tattoos.

Spittle wells in the sharp corners of his mouth and jets out with the poison of his words.

The poetry he spins is black and bitter with the shit of the city, clammy with sex, haunted by death. Shadowboxing and sidewinding, his movements are mesmeric.

The legendary Whiskey A Go Go smacks of girls and liquor but tonight's thrill is live naked rock 'n' roll. Guns N' Roses are pissing raw depravity up the club's clean brick-face walls.

Saw-toothed riffs recall the greatest gut rock. AC/DC, Aerosmith, the Rolling Stones, Sex Pistols, Led Zeppelin, Hanoi Rocks. A shrieky, spluttering sound mix rattles but can't jam their motor.

"Ain't my fault the PA sucks!" spits Axl; which is as near as this band gets to apologising.

Feeding off wild adrenalin and whatever else comes to hand, Guns N' Roses rip and tear through the meat of their soon-to-be-released debut album *Appetite For Destruction*. 'You're Crazy', 'Nightrain', 'My

Slash with the devil's right hand, the Gibson Les Paul.

Michelle'. Bullets from a misfit's heart, anthems to the estranged.

The set comes to a violent end, they shoot surly thanks and exit. Guns N' Roses quit the Whiskey having proved themselves the most intoxicating hard rock 'n' roll band in the world.

Two road years later, Guns return to Los Angeles as the people's rock 'n' roll band of the late Eighties and early Nineties.

LA Guns 'N' Hollywood Roses

WAxl Rose, Izzy Stradlin', Duff McKagan, Steven Adler and Slash played their first gig together as Guns N' Roses at The Troubadour, a smallish club in Los Angeles.

"It was a Thursday night," says Slash. "I'd rehearsed with the band for two days."

"As of June '85," adds Axl, "*this* was Guns N' Roses."

Individually, the band give confused accounts of the events leading up to that legendary Thursday night. The past is perhaps blurred by too much Night Train.

The original Guns N' Roses featured Axl, Izzy, Duff, Rob Gardner and Tracii Guns. It was early '85. Axl and Izzy had been in LA for three years, sleeping rough. Duff was fresh out of Seattle.

The name Guns N' Roses was a hybrid of LA Guns and Hollywood Roses, two bands in which various members were involved. Before settling on GN'R, they'd dreamt up a string of bizarre names, including AIDS and Heads Of Amazon.

When, in May of '85, Rob and Tracii dragged their feet at the prospect of a club tour that Duff had set up along the West Coast, Slash and Steven were called up at Duff's suggestion. Slash and Steven were the existing two-man nucleus of a spluttering local band, Road Crew, which Duff had spent a short time playing bass for.

Exit Rob and Tracii, the latter to reform LA Guns.

Strangely, Axl refers in an early interview to playing a gig "with Slash and Steve in Hollywood Rose," a band which the other two fail to mention. In addition, Duff claims that it was he who "told Axl about Slash and Steven."

Even the chronology is muddled. If Slash and Steven were drafted for a West Coast tour, was the Troubadour debut simply a warm-up show? Only Guns N' Roses themselves

Guns N' Roses; an early study. Just another day in Paradise City.

know the answers to these mysteries. And they can't remember!

Perversely, they each have total recall of their squalid early communal band lifestyle. The big neon glitz of Los Angeles had sucked them in like flies and, as Izzy succinctly puts it, "we had to eat shit to get where we are!"

Before signing to Geffen, Guns N' Roses lived hand-to-mouth.

"We tried to live on $3.75 a day," reveals Axl, "which was enough to buy biscuits and gravy at Denny's for a buck and a quarter, a bottle of Night Train for a buck and a quarter, or some really cheap wine like Thunderbird. That's it. We survived. Even if you were dead tired you made a party."

All five of the band slept wherever they could in a ramshackle studio

> "That's it. We survived. Even if you were dead tired you made a party."

apartment in Hollywood. It was dubbed The Hellhouse, "but God," beams Slash, "did we sound good in there!"

"We tried to get as many girls into the loft as we could. I don't know. It got pretty wild. There was a lot of indoor and outdoor sex. We were living there when we got signed and every one of us was broke at the time."

The band also lived for a short time at the West Hollywood apartment of their first manager, Vicky Hamilton. Into one large room they crammed amps, guitars, clothes, bodies, any old rubbish. Vicky had recently helped put Poison's cheap glam cabaret into America's stadia.

"She doesn't get to pay her rent," said Slash at the time, "'cause she spends all the money she can possibly get her hands on trying to get us off the ground."

The band's sole means of support was, Steven laughs, "G.I.R.L.S."

"We sold drugs," drawls Izzy, "sold girls. We *managed*. In the beginning we'd throw parties and ransack the girl's purse while one of the guys was with her."

"Not being sexist or anything," adds Slash, clumsily, "it's fucking amazing how much abuse girls will take! At one point, most of us had girlfriends, but as soon as the band started happening — goodbye.

They're a pain in the ass. They take up too much time and they have their own ideas which they're constantly throwing in your face."

"At that point in my career it was easier for me not to have a girlfriend," reasons Axl. "Besides, I didn't have the money to support a girlfriend. And they got tired of having to take you to dinner every day."

"We love to take care of women," insists Steve, "we love to treat them great. But we didn't have any money then, so we treated 'em like shit."

Guns N' Roses played LA's notorious dives — The Whiskey, The Roxy, The Troubadour, Scream.

"Their draw," explained Vicky back in '86, "went from 150 to 700 almost overnight. I think it was their friends networking more than anything. It was word-of-mouth, not advertising.

Says Axl: "As soon as we began headlining we brought in different opening bands like Jetboy, Faster Pussycat and LA Guns, and it kinda created this scene. In that crowd we were pretty much the top draw.

"It didn't have a shower," continues Axl. "And the rain always leaked in. I once stole this wood and we built this loft so we could have a place to sleep above our equipment. We tried to get as many girls into the loft as we could. I don't know. It got pretty wild. There was a lot of indoor and outdoor sex. We were living there when we got signed and every one of us was broke at the time."

"She doesn't get to pay her rent," said Slash at the time, "'cause she spends all the money she can possibly get her hands on trying to get us off the ground."

Izzy in the hungry years.

bands out. We always tried to help others 'cause I wanna see a really cool rock scene. I wanna be able to turn on my radio and not be sick about the shit I'm gonna hear."

"The thought of the LA scene just made me sick," sneers Slash. "LA is considered a pretty gay place and we got a lotta flak from people thinkin' we were posers."

"Poison fucked it up for all of us," griped Axl. "They said that everyone in LA was following *their* trend! I've told those guys personally that they can lock me in a room with all of them and I'll be the only one who walks out!"

Having flirted for months on end with several record companies as a means of dining out for free, Guns N' Roses finally signed to Geffen Records on 25 March 1986. Soon after, Guns split with Vicky Hamilton.

Tom Zutaut and Teresa Ensenat, the A&R team who'd procured Guns N' Roses for Geffen, then spent several frantic months seeking out a new manager for the band. Zutaut brought Aerosmith manager Tim Collins to LA for a showcase gig. Afterwards, the band ran up a 400-dollar drinks tab on Collins' hotel bill when he'd checked into a second room in order to get some sleep. By the morning, Collins decided he'd seen enough.

In August Englishman Alan Niven was hired as Guns N' Roses manager. At that point $100,000 had been spent on recording for the band's first album and there was no usable material in the can. Niven, so the legend on *Appetite For Destruction*'s inner sleeve goes, came in and kicked ass when it was needed.

Eventually, we quit playing for a while to work on the record *Appetite For Destruction* and the others started headlining, but some of them weren't as cool about helping other

W. AXL ROSE

Rock outlaw archetype. Bleeding heart romantic. Jail-bird. Desperado. Loner. Manic depressive. Junk fiend. One bad, dog-slayin' mother. Dirt with an angel face. A brawler. A bigot. A corpse.

Rumour has nailed W Axl Rose as amoral, schizoid, petulant, out of control, even dead. Axl's not dead. He shot a pig, not a whole pack of dogs. But there is a core of truth amid the other rumours, given that each story is inevitably fleshed out with a little cheap sensationalism.

"Axl," joked Slash back in 1986, "is just another version of The Ayatollah!"

It's a lazy, throwaway caricature, but it says something of Axl's fire and will to lead.

Guns N' Roses' uncompromising vocalist has followed his own heart and stubborn convictions from an early age. Born 6 February 1962 in Lafayette, Indiana, he was raised as Bill Bailey, eldest son of L. Stephen and Sharon Bailey.

Aged 17 and bored of smalltown mid-America, Bill began wearing his red-bronze hair long, singing in local garage bands, clashing with his parents.

He was all mouth, angst and spunk when he suddenly discovered his hitherto secret past. L. Stephen Bailey was in fact his stepfather. His surname at birth was indeed Rose, and his natural father – a wrecker and rolling stone, whose current whereabouts are unknown – upped and left Sharon when Bill was little more than a babe-in-arms.

Bill exploded with confused anger. He re-christened himself W Rose and his frustrations were expressed in a classic case history of juvenile delinquency. Adding to his new name that of Axl, a band in which he had sung, Rose was soon familiar with the Lafayette police cells.

"I got thrown in jail over 20 times," he recalls bitterly, "and five of those times I was guilty. Of what? Public consumption – I was drinking at a party under-age. The other times I got busted 'cos the cops hated me. So I don't have much love for that fucking place!"

Now less angry than before, Axl regards his stepfather as his "real dad". Nevertheless, he legally changed his name to W Axl Rose shortly before Guns N' Roses signed their recording contract with the Geffen label in March of 1986.

"Axl," joked Slash back in 1986, "is just another version of The Ayatollah!"

Axl possesses at least "five or six different voices". His temperament is equally volatile.

Psychiatrists have clinically diagnosed his condition as a manic-depressive disorder, which is prevalent among individuals of exceptional ability. Axl struggles to contain his "mood swings" with the aid of Lithium.

"I'm very sensitive and emotional. Things upset me and make me feel like not functioning or dealing with people, the band or anything.

"I went to a clinic thinking it would help my moods. The only thing I did was take one 500-question test – y'know, filling in all the little black dots. All of a sudden I'm diagnosed manic-depressive!

"'Let's put Axl on medication'. Well, the medication doesn't help me deal with stress. The only thing it does is

W. Axl Rose. One bad mother.

help keep people off my back because they figure I'm on medication."

Axl's psychosis was also noted back in Indiana by a close friend, Jeff Isabelle; another of Lafayette's wild ones, now better known as Izzy Stradlin'.

"He was a serious lunatic when I met him," remembers Izzy, "really fucking bent on fighting and destroying things."

As Izzy sees it, rock 'n' roll, specifically Guns N' Roses, is Axl's salvation.

"If it wasn't for the band, I just hate to think what he'd have done."

"I go crazy," Axl confesses. "I clear a club if an argument starts. Slash has a way of working things out a bit and avoiding trouble as much as possible. He seems to slip into corners and he doesn't know how he does it. *I'm* right in someone's face saying, 'What do you *mean* we can't have more beer?'"

The flipside to this bilious and self-destructive aggression is the quiet intensity which is mirrored in the simple, soul-baring romanticism of 'Patience' or 'Sweet Child O' Mine'. Axl is a great conversationalist. After shows, he'll talk till past sunrise with assorted hangers-on, or he'll just slip away quietly and lock himself behind that night's hotel room door.

Before the band's success sky-rocketed, it was principally Axl who harangued the world's press with the hardline according to Guns N' Roses. He's a sharp and garrulous interviewee, his voice soft, deep, slightly rasping, his hands a flurry of gestures. Now, misquoted and misinterpreted, he rarely opens up to the media.

It's from a stage that he can truly communicate.

"I live for the songs. If I go through a bad time, well, anything I have to go through is worth it if I've got a song out of it."

"If I had to sleep in a parking garage and hated it but got a song out of the experience, I'm glad that I had to go through a ton of shit – I've got a bitchin' song."

"When I'm onstage, that's when I get to take what I'm worth to the public. When I'm singing a line, I'm thinking of the feelings that made me come up with the song in the first place. At the same time, I think about how I feel singing those words now, and how those words are gonna hit people in the crowd.

"I usually have to have someone stand beside me when I come off stage because I can't really even tie my own shoes, I've gone through so many thoughts on stage."

Pre-album Los Angeles club shows were especially fraught.

"You look out at a crowd of 700 people and you know 300 of them. This person loves you, this one hates you and this one's mad at you because you owe him five bucks and you're mad at another guy 'cause he owes you 25."

"You see all this stuff, plus you're thinking about the feelings in the music. I try to put every single thought I possibly can into every performance and every line. And that's why I might be known as histrionic, 'cause I go full out."

Dallas 1988. The band offstage and on.

"If you're bored of a song and it's one of your songs, you just play it. It's like having a pair of pants. Those pants meant something to you at one time – you liked 'em or whatever – but you just outgrow 'em, you're tired of wearing them, and they're not you anymore. Some songs I rewrite 'cause the verses aren't me anymore.

"I can come off the stage in tears because I was so moved by the music. I want people to feel that too.

"In my life as a singer there have been a few times when I've gone into a trance while I'm singing and have come to as if I'd been knocked out on the floor, because I was so far into the song. There's been a couple of times while singing 'You're Crazy' when I've got lost in the song and then found I was almost ready to fall off the stage! I try to throw myself into the song that much every time. I really don't feel like I'm breaking free of my emotions. I feel like I'm trying to."

As Bill Bailey and as W Axl Rose, life has been a struggle for self-expression. Broken hearts, busted jaws; it's all inspiration.

"I explore emotional situations of any kind – with a lover, a friend – and try to put it into the best words I can. Something good or tragic, something that moves me so much that my mind can't seem to escape."

When Guns N' Roses toured America with Aerosmith in the summer of 1989, fevered reports of Axl's alleged death circulated at the rate of at least one per week. The craziest story claimed that Slash had shot the singer dead!

Slash and firearms are the least of Axl's worries. Two weeks prior to Guns N' Roses first UK shows at London's Marquee club in June 1987, Axl lay under electrodes in a Los Angeles hospital's intensive care unit. Yes, it was that close.

Axl is reckless, but where Izzy and Slash sank body and soul into the hell of heroin addiction, Axl never lost control.

A high-IQ hellraiser with a liver of granite and a bruised rock 'n' roll heart on his sleeve, Axl is strong, sensitive too, but wildly unpredictable, even to those he's lived, loved and worked with for years.

"He can still be a tyrant," admits Izzy, "but then he can turn around and be the nicest guy in the world."

'He does a lotta weird shit that no-one understands," shrugs Slash, "But I love the guy. He's a sweetheart, and the most temperamental fucking meanest little fuck in the world!"

ANOTHER ROCK 'N' ROLL SUICIDE

" I don't care if you think I've got a bad attitude or if I'm being big-headed about it," blurted Slash back in '86, "This is the only rock 'n' roll band to come out of LA that's real and the kids know it."

"They haven't seen anything like it in the last ten years," concludes Axl. "Van Halen was the last real rock 'n' roll band out of LA."

"Mötley Crüe was more teen-metal," decides Izzy. "We go for a more roots-oriented sound."

Guns N' Roses first came to wide-

> "This is the only rock 'n' roll band to come out of LA that's real and the kids know it."

spread notoriety in 1986 with the release of their first EP, *Live ?!*@ *Like A Suicide*, a four-tracker issued on their own Uzi Suicide label. *Suicide* brought to the world Guns N'

Roses live, ragged, uncensored. The band were declared natural successors to the legendary Aerosmith, who stood for 15 years as the definitive American rock 'n' roll band. The connection was inevitable given that *Suicide* numbered amongst its tracks a cover of Aerosmith's 'Mama Kin'.

"In my mind," said Axl, "the hardest, ballsiest rock band that ever came out of America was Aerosmith. What I always liked about 'em was that they weren't the guys you'd want to meet at the end of an alley if you'd had a disagreement. I always wanted to come out of America with that same attitude.

"So, one reason why there's been this Aerosmith comparison is, fuck, they were the only goddam role model to come out of here! They were a tradition that I grew up with. They were the only band that people who lived in my city in Indiana would accept wearing make-up and dress-ing cool. These people thought the Stones were fags, but everybody liked Aerosmith. We are influenced by them but it goes deeper than that in that we're also influenced by some of the things they're influenced by, like Muddy Waters, Howlin' Wolf, old blues things, black artists."

Less flatteringly, Guns N' Roses

were frequently dismissed as just another year's model of the perennial badass LA crotch-rock band.

Argued Slash: "The only reason we get that bad-boy shit is because the other bands in LA are such wimps!"

GN'R were even tarred 'glam', no doubt as a reference to the kitsch scarves worn by Steven and Slash in the EP's rear sleeve photograph.

"We don' know what glam is," sulked Izzy at the time.

"Glam," spat Axl, "reminds me of bands like Angel who rely more on fashion than their music."

"If I had to label this band," grumbled Slash, "I'd say that it's a hard rock band with an R&B base. It's not a glam band, not a heavy metal band, not a country band."

"We listen to funk, disco, metal, classical," explained Axl. "We listen to soundtracks, old Fifties stuff, Sixties music."

"We're influenced by all of it. We're not doing anything that I would call original, it's all been done before."

"We're not doing anything new – we're just trying to be as sincere as we can with our music and just put it out the best way we can. In other words, all our songs ain't gonna be mellow, they're gonna have a heavy edge to them."

Live ?!@ *Like A Suicide* mixes two cover versions with two GN'R originals. The second is a frenetic run through Rose Tattoo's 'Nice Boys', a cut from the now-defunct Australian quintet's *Rock 'N' Roll Outlaws*.

The original songs are seedy autobiographies: 'Reckless Life' ("it's my only vice"), born of arrogant, masochistic abandon, and 'Move To The City', straight from Izzy and Axl's gypsy hearts. Guns N' Roses dedicated *Suicide* "to all the people who have helped keep us alive"; "to our friends," according to the sleeve, "for support in the streets as well as the stage."

Explained Izzy: "We felt that all the people who saw us from the beginning should have a chance to get our early stuff on record. So we only printed up 10,000 copies. That way, they can feel they have a special limited edition. It's like an expensive dedication to all the kids who helped us get going when we had no money."

The EP also served as a stop-gap. When *Suicide* hit the streets, *Appetite For Destruction* was recorded and mixed but wasn't due for release for another six months.

STEVEN ADLER

"I'm from Hollywood. Born and raised in America."

Steven Adler was born 22 January 1965 in Cleveland, Ohio, but is the living, breathing essence of California. Sun-dried ash blond, tanned, slim, blue-eyed and carefree. Steven was a teenage Kiss freak and is in many ways still the same easygoing and purely hedonistic beach bum who at 15 got Slash hip to the electric guitar.

Drums were not Steven's first love but when, at around 17, he figured his guitar playing wasn't working out so well, he took to beating on pots and pans and saving for a full-blown drum kit. At one point, fearing he'd never scrape together enough money, Steven hit on the idea of singing. Briefly and without success, he fronted one of many low-key Hollywood garage bands that Slash was working on.

Stung by failure, Steven quit singing and got back to the serious business of playing drums. Slash was in a band named Road Crew – "the first real musical thing I had that actually went out and played at high schools and parties" – when all of a sudden, the guitarist remembers:

"Steven showed up one day and said, 'Get rid of your drummer, he's not good enough.'"

Steven had somehow got his hands on a kit and he'd gotten good. Me and Steven carried Road Crew on, which was a great little band. Sorta like what Metallica are now without a singer."

Steven's drumming is direct and sweats hard, dispensing with flash and frills. Likewise, he's portrayed by those around him as an exuberant personality, big-hearted and of simple tastes. In the industry's working vernacular, Steven lives to play rock 'n' roll and get his dick sucked.

An early interview, printed in a Los Angeles-based periodical prior to the band signing to Geffen, asked each of Guns N' Roses to name their one greatest wish.

Steven Adler, aka Mr. Lewis Cipher: I was a teenage Kiss freak.

Slash craved "a constant supply of Marlboros," Izzy a "Maserati four-wheel drive." Duff wished the first record was released and the band were out on the road. Axl, difficult again, wanted "all the wishes there are to have." Steven simply sought "peace of mind."

Amid the madness of a megabuck rock 'n' roll tour, Steven could hardly be more relaxed. Before a show at a sold-out 15,000-capacity Texan arena, he saunters about the dressing room, idly talking and laughing, rattling his sticks on flightcases and slurping down vials of syrupy royal jelly. "Builds up come in your balls!" he gurgles.

Steven. A born celebrity.

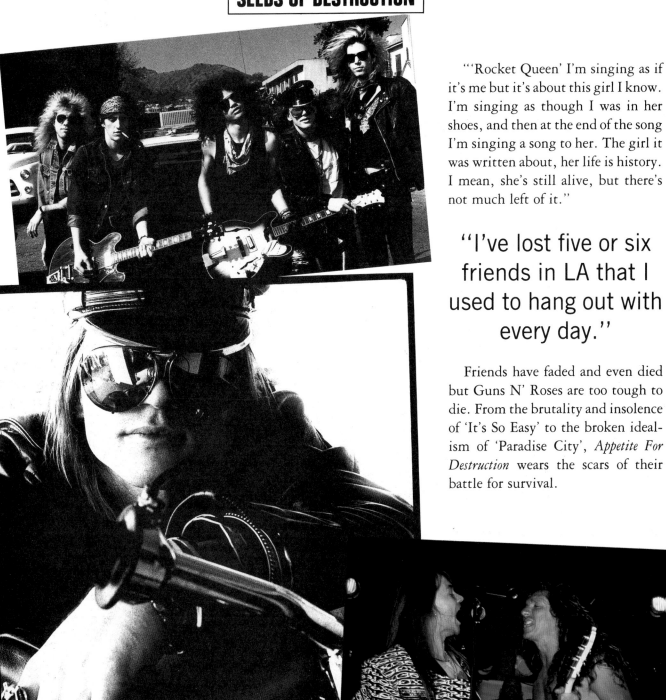

"'Rocket Queen' I'm singing as if it's me but it's about this girl I know. I'm singing as though I was in her shoes, and then at the end of the song I'm singing a song to her. The girl it was written about, her life is history. I mean, she's still alive, but there's not much left of it.''

"I've lost five or six friends in LA that I used to hang out with every day.''

Friends have faded and even died but Guns N' Roses are too tough to die. From the brutality and insolence of 'It's So Easy' to the broken idealism of 'Paradise City', *Appetite For Destruction* wears the scars of their battle for survival.

Above: **Axl joins former Sex Pistol Steve Jones on stage. The Pistols are a big influence on Guns N' Roses. Axl and Jones are now good friends.**

Los Angeles, March 1987. The killer rock 'n' roll album of the 1980s is fresh in the can.

in the face of the Indiana and Los Angeles police; "The West Hollywood sheriffs," remarked a weary Izzy upon the album's release, "have gotta be the biggest fucking pigfaces I've ever known!"

'Nightrain' glorifies GN'R's favourite cheap killer wine – "you drink a quarter," says Axl, "and you black out" – while 'Mr Brownstone' tells the inside story on heroin addiction. Says Slash: "There was a point where I stopped playing guitar and didn't even talk to my band, except for Izzy, 'cause we were both doing it. I didn't come out of my apartment for three months, except to go to the market. The one thing that really stopped me was a phone call from Duff, saying, 'You've alienated yourself from everybody'. Since they're the only people I'm really close to, that really affected me, and I quit."

"I didn't come out of my apartment for three months, except to go to the market."

'Sweet Child O'Mine' was written for Axl's girlfriend Erin, daughter of Everly Brother Don. 'Rocket Queen' and 'My Michelle' are also real life stories of girls whom Axl has known.

"When I first wrote 'My Michelle'," remembers Axl. "I'd written it all nice and I thought, that's not how it really is. So I wrote the real story down, kind of as a joke. She and her dad ended up loving it. It's a true story – I met her when I was 13 and went out with her later – and that's what works, I think.

31

SEEDS OF DESTRUCTION

I n the Spring of 1987, Guns N' Roses had left The Hellhouse and were receiving their routine LAPD calls at a new band residence – a smallish, beat-up wooden bungalow off Santa Monica Boulevard, its white paintwork flaking, its driveway and lawn overflowing with both working and rotting automobiles.

Amid shabby furniture, piles of clothes, guitars, speaker cabs and sacks of garbage lay the seeds of destruction, the scratchy old records that fired the band's collective imagination. Plenty of Rolling Stones, Aerosmith, Sex Pistols, Metallica, Ramones, Misfits, Queen, Led Zeppelin, AC/DC, Bo Diddley.

"In one year I spent over 1300 dollars on cassettes, everything from Slayer to Wham!, to listen to production, vocals, melodies, this and that," reveals Axl. "I'm from Indiana where Lynyrd Skynyrd are considered God to the point that you end up saying, I hate this fucking band! And yet for our song 'Sweet Child O' Mine' I went out and got some old Lynyrd Skynyrd tapes to make sure that we'd got that downhome, heartfelt feeling."

Appetite For Destruction was released worldwide on 31 July 1987.

"In one year I spent over 1300 dollars on cassettes, everything from Slayer to Wham!"

When hired, producer Mike Clink wasn't a big name, but the last thing Guns N' Roses needed was a prima donna at the mixing desk. Clink had two qualifications: "great guitar sounds and a tremendous amount of patience." His brief was to transfer to flat tape all the new emotion that had burned inside the members of Guns N' Roses for 20, 25 years. He got it all: rage, paranoia, lust, spite, love.

Like 'Move To The City' before it, 'Welcome To The Jungle' shivers with the cold sweat of a country boy cut loose in the big city. In the promo video, Axl plays the saucer-eyed hick, Izzy the great shark. 'Out Ta Get Me', dedicated at the Marquee to the band's critics, blows up

Diary of a road hog.

Steven Adler is a born celebrity. He gets a kick out of the star trip but deals with the glitz and the hubbub on the most straightforward level. He loves to sign autographs and just hasn't the heart to say no to an on-stage jam; more recently, he goofed off with Bon Jovi in San Diego.

Given the popular assumption that people who hit things for a living are inevitably weak of mind, Steven has been branded shallow by some who've come into brief contact with him. While this may be a consequence of his boyish sense of fun, it's also apparent that the media generally hang on a singer's every word while dismissing those of a drummer as mere small talk.

This isn't so. Off the cuff, Steven crystallises the Los Angeles bullshit rock society in a single sentence.

"In LA, there's a million people who think they're

musicians and only a few who are."

During breaks in touring Steven rehearses and refines new material mainly with Duff and Slash. And on 3 June 1989, he wed his longtime girlfriend Cheryl in Las Vegas.

However, it's on the road that Steven, like Slash, feels truly at ease. His appetite for touring is such that he even asked manager Alan Niven if he could roadie for another of Niven's charges, Great White, as a means of getting back out on the open road.

Known to hotels the world over as Mr Lewis Cipher, Steven Adler is a certifiable road hog with an itch that two solid years of touring couldn't scratch. He and Slash will never be genuinely happy unless there's a new album in the stores and Guns N' Roses are riding out the road and air miles on sweat and adrenalin.

Steven. A born celebrity.

"Steven showed up one day and said, 'Get rid of your drummer, he's not good enough.'"

Steven had somehow got his hands on a kit and he'd gotten good. Me and Steven carried Road Crew on, which was a great little band. Sorta like what Metallica are now without a singer."

Steven's drumming is direct and sweats hard, dispensing with flash and frills. Likewise, he's portrayed by those around him as an exuberant personality, big-hearted and of simple tastes. In the industry's working vernacular, Steven lives to play rock 'n' roll and get his dick sucked.

An early interview, printed in a Los Angeles-based periodical prior to the band signing to Geffen, asked each of Guns N' Roses to name their one greatest wish.

Steven Adler, aka Mr. Lewis Cipher: I was a teenage Kiss freak.

Slash craved "a constant supply of Marlboros," Izzy a "Maserati four-wheel drive." Duff wished the first record was released and the band were out on the road. Axl, difficult again, wanted "all the wishes there are to have." Steven simply sought "peace of mind."

Amid the madness of a megabuck rock 'n' roll tour, Steven could hardly be more relaxed. Before a show at a sold-out 15,000-capacity Texan arena, he saunters about the dressing room, idly talking and laughing, rattling his sticks on flightcases and slurping down vials of syrupy royal jelly. "Builds up come in your balls!" he gurgles.

Summer in Soho

" It's good to be in fucking England finally," Axl half purrs, half hisses. Guns N' Roses can at last dig their heels into the stage of London's famous old Marquee club in Soho's Wardour Street.

But a bristling crowd isn't about to let LA's new big thing just roll into London unchallenged. Rattling through 'Reckless Life' and 'Out Ta Get Me', Guns N' Roses are met with a hail of plastic beerglasses. Phlegm from the first few rows sticks and hangs in Izzy and Axl's hair. Axl's hackles rise.

"Hey! If you wanna keep throwin' things we're gonna fuckin' leave! Whaddaya think?"

Another glass clatters into Steven's cymbals.

"Hey!" Axl boils. "Fuck you, pussy!"

The barrage slows to a trickle by the end of the third song, 'Anything Goes'. Guns N' Roses have won out.

The month which Guns N' Roses spent on the streets of London in the summer of '87 stank of controversy. They rode into Britain on a bad reputation; even on the Los Angeles–London flight, a drunk Slash all but burnt his own ass off slumbering in a

Guns N' Roses are met with a hail of plastic beerglasses. Phlegm from the first few rows sticks and hangs in Izzy and Axl's hair.

The Marquee, Soho, London; 19 June 1987.

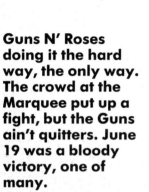

Guns N' Roses doing it the hard way, the only way. The crowd at the Marquee put up a fight, but the Guns ain't quitters. June 19 was a bloody victory, one of many.

seat that he'd unwittingly set on fire with a cigarette!

"A rock band even nastier than the Beastie Boys is heading for Britain," quaked the *Star* newspaper. "Los Angeles-based Guns N' Roses are led by the outrageous Axl Rose, who has an endearing habit of butchering dogs. Record company bosses are already worried that Rose's hatred of dogs could cause a backlash amongst animal lovers. He is on record as saying: 'I have a personal disgust for small dogs, like poodles. Everything about them means I must kill them.' The other two [!] members of the group are as sleazy as their crackpot

leader. Guitarist Slash and bass player Duff McKagan claim they have been on a boozing binge for TWO YEARS. Says Slash: 'When we get up in the afternoon we can't play because our hands are shaking like windmills.'"

Axl was joking, Slash was exaggerating, but the reputation stuck. The *Star* also reported that in an

"I have a personal disgust for small dogs, like poodles. Everything about them means I must kill them."

earlier incident back on the West Coast, Axl had been hospitalised "for three days after a vicious battle with LA police." Axl himself gave a muddled account of the incident.

"It just kinda happened real quickly. I got hit on the head by a cop and I guess I just blacked out. Two days later I woke up in hospital tied to the bed with electrodes over

me. I guess they had to give me electro-shock. I don't know a whole lot about what happened."

Back then, the party was never over for Axl till police or paramedics rolled up. Had he not been admitted to hospital so quickly, Guns N' Roses might never have made it out of Los Angeles.

Trouble, it seemed, lurked at every corner. "Y'know," shrugged Axl at the first Marquee gig, "we just got here, right? I go to Tower Rec-

"Two days later I woke up in hospital tied to the bed with electrodes over me."

ords, I sit down, and the security throw me out. And then they call the local constables – ain't that what they call 'em? And they were a coupla right dickheads. They'll be getting

letters to their bosses, a nice little write-up."

Axl, accompanied by Alan Niven and Tom Zutaut of Geffen Records, had gone late one night to the Tower Records store at Piccadilly Circus. Drowsy with jet-lag and the side effects of an anti-histamine drug he'd taken to break up some congestion, Axl sat on a step in Tower's cassette department, where he had just bought an Eagles tape. Three large members of the store's security staff

allegedly pulled him up without first showing their ID. An ugly shouting match and the inevitable jostling ensued. Eventually the police were called to intervene.

"The cops are kinda different here," reflected Axl. "When they turned up at Tower, Alan [Niven] said to 'em, 'Take your hands off me!' And they did! Back in LA, they won't take any of that shit. You'd be slung straight across the front of the squad car with a gun to your head!"

Guns N' Roses played three shows at the Marquee – 19, 22 and 28 June – each one better than the last.

"The crowd were so fuckin' into it," Axl smiled. "So much energy. They threw some shit to start with but they cooled it after a while. But shit, it was hot in there! Real hard to breathe. Steven lost about ten pounds in weight during each show. I'd got out of hospital only a week before the first show. When we started that show it was like, man, we're in hell!"

Axl left London with some popular myths exploded – "English beer ain't that fuckin' warm!" – and others still a mystery: "what the fuck is

Spotted Dick? I can't believe you eat this thing called Spotted Dick!"

Guns N' Roses entered Britain with the reputation of sex-crazed, booze-sodden, drug-dealin' dog-killers. They left with a reputation as the most electrifying live rock 'n' roll band on the planet.

"D'ya like my shirt?" grinned Axl at the Marquee. "It says, 'Fuck Dancing, Let's Fuck!' I think that gets to the point!"

So had Guns N' Roses.

June 1987. Izzy and Slash hold up their weary, drunken frames for the British music press at the Soho offices of WEA Records, just a whisky bottle's throw from the Marquee.

SLASH

Two knocks at the door are followed by a thin voice.

"Message for Mr Peter Cottontail."

There are no cartoon rabbits in. Only an off-duty rock guitarist, wet from a shower, towel clinging to his waist, damp hair veiling his dark eyes and a large tumbler of Jack Daniel's in one hand. Slash peers round the door and takes the slip of paper from the bemused hotel porter.

He chuckles over another sleazy birthday greeting. Slash has just turned 23 – 'HAPPY FUCKIN' BIRTHDAY, YOU FUCKER!' spat the cake icing. It's Dallas, Texas, 23 July 1988. The gig is tomorrow night and Slash's liver and testicles are braced for a long, hard night of celebration.

Slash lives for the road.

"Ozzy Osborne is someone I can relate to," he explains. "His life is so rock 'n' roll oriented. He doesn't have anything else. That's the way I feel."

Slash was born Saul Hudson in Stoke-on-Trent, England, in 1965 ("Stock-In-Trent," he once mis-spelt it). His parents were an interracial couple who split when Slash was still young. His father, Anthony Hudson, designed album covers, notably Joni Mitchell's *Court And Spark*. His mother Ola was a costume artist. She designed David Bowie's clothing for the 1975 futuristic shocker, *The Man Who Fell To Earth*. A friend of his father's hit on the nickname Slash.

"When I was in England, I was very strange because I was the only kid with long hair. I was given lots of freedom as a kid. I grew up in a kind of rebellious hippy household. I started saying the word 'fuck' when I was like seven or eight years old, telling my parents to fuck off!

Slash is 23 today. The cake says it all.

> "Ozzy Osborne is someone I can relate to," he explains. "His life is so rock 'n' roll oriented. He doesn't have anything else. That's the way I feel."

"They were always very attentive, and I don't have any problems with my family, nothing at all compared to a lot of musicians who complain about getting kicked out of the house because they grew their hair, or were told to 'Fuck off and get a job'. I never had that. I've always been pretty rebellious, to teachers, cops and the like, but my family, my childhood, that was pretty cool."

In 1976, Anthony Hudson emigrated with his son to

Hollywood. Slash, 11 years old, struggled a little in adjusting to his new life.

"When I came to LA and started school, I never really fitted in. I didn't really have a group of friends. Then, when I was 13 years old, I just thought, fuck it, and didn't worry about it anymore. Then all of a sudden everybody was cool, and I started becoming popular. It was really strange, but I didn't really care by then because I was into hanging out by myself, ditching school and practising guitar. And then, all of a sudden, I started getting lots of girlfriends.

"There was music in my house all my life. I never planned or aspired to be a musician or anything, I just loved music."

Slash got hooked on the idea of playing guitar while hanging out with a friend he'd stumbled upon at high school, Steven Adler.

"He had a guitar and an amp and he'd just plug in and turn it up all the way up and bang on it real loud. And I was just fucking fascinated with it.

"Most guitarists start playing guitar to get laid, to look cool or to get some heavy image. I started playing guitar out of ignorance, because I wanted to play an instrument that was rock 'n' roll orientated, but I didn't know back then the difference between bass and lead guitar or any of that shit! I basically chose the guitar because it had more strings!

Right: Soundcheck, Dallas 1988. A lazy afternoon jam with Izzy, Duff and Steven.

"There was music in my house all my life. I never planned or aspired to be a musician or anything, I just loved music."

"I don't think of it as a phallic symbol. I don't think it's a symbol of anything. Basically, as far as what I use a guitar for, it's just something to hide behind, because I'm quite shy."

Softly spoken, Slash is more introverted than his whiplash guitar playing and arrogant stage demeanour suggest.

"I'm not nervous on stage. I get into being up there, it's this huge energy release. When I'm up on stage, that's my element. But I avoid eye contact. I've also got my guitar to hide behind.

"I'm completely in my own world up there. I couldn't be a lead singer, there's no way I could do that."

A guitar isn't his sole mask. There's the tangle of corkscrew hair shading his eyes; then there's the omnipresent bottle of sour mash. . . .

"If I don't have a drink I sink into myself. And I like it! I like being drunk, it's fun. It's a habit I picked up when I was 12 years old. It helps me, it brings me out of my shell. I can't deal with people in a social situation when I'm sober.

"I'm usually quite a good drinker, though I admit I can get a bit obnoxious when I'm drunk sometimes. I'm one of those blackout drunks. I get so fucked up I don't remember anything. I probably give the impression of being a real asshole most of the time, but I'm not really that bad."

Slash and Jack: the best of friends.

Dallas 1988. Uncompromising as ever, Guns N' Roses ate up 10–15 minutes of a 45-minute set with a rambling blues improvisation. Here, Slash cuts loose.

"I probably give the impression of being a real asshole most of the time, but I'm not really that bad."

He is, however, prey to more serious indulgences. In the early part of 1989, Guns N' Roses were forced to quit Iron Maiden's US tour. Holed up in LA with idle hands and surplus adrenalin, Slash succumbed wholly to booze and narcotics. Alarmed at this wanton self-abuse, Alan Niven packed Slash off on a purging vacation.

The guitarist was lured to Niven's management office, ostensibly for the purpose of a press interview, and was immediately bundled on to the first available flight to Hawaii.

"All in all I can't say that it hurt me. I took vitamins for, like, eight days, didn't drink that much, got a suntan. I hadn't been out of a pair of black jeans since I was about 14! I was getting ingrowing hairs on my legs!"

Izzy reckons Slash had "really stepped off the edge".

"Yeah," Slash nods, "and I didn't want to do anything that'd hurt the band, so I spent eight days in fuckin' hell!"

On another occasion, Slash was nursed through heroin withdrawal for days and nights on end by Niven and his wife. Once clean, Slash disappeared from Niven's home and wound up wasted again by the next day.

Slash invited porn star Tracy Lords to America's MTV music awards ceremony in January of 1989, but only for the hell of it. It ain't love.

"The situation with women is completely fucked up because all the girls you run into that are interested in you are usually interested because you're in a band. And that tends to be pretty, er, I don't know, pretty *low*.

"It gets a little bit lonely. There's been a real downside to all this success. I'm only just realising it. I don't go out that much. I don't have that many close friends. And what close friends I have, the time I get to see them are usually few and far between."

A life on the road is both cause and cure of Slash's loneliness.

At his new home in the Hollywood hills, its decor heavy with purple and black and hung tapestries, Slash

> "I took vitamins for, like, eight days, didn't drink that much, got a suntan. I hadn't been out of a pair of black jeans since I was about 14! I was getting ingrowing hairs on my legs!"

has just his snakes for company. He owns ten snakes (boas and pythons), some of which are almost 14 feet long. They are housed in a customised serpentarium and fed on just about anything small, furry and alive.

On a tour there's less time to be lonely. There is always a score, a bottle and a girl waiting.

"Real sex," slurred Slash the morning after the night in Dallas, "is so hard to come by. But last night was cool. We got into this great position so this chick could watch in the reflection of the wardrobe mirror as I was screwing her. Pretty good birthday . . .".

Real sex; the afterglow.

THE TRAIL
OF DESTRUCTION

Within four months of the Marquee gigs, Guns N' Roses were back in Britain. In chill, rain-lashed Manchester, Axl acquired a bizarre souvenir from a Scottish fan. It was a concert ticket for a show that never was: Aerosmith at the Edinburgh Playhouse, supported by Guns N' Roses.

Aerosmith cancelled the proposed UK leg of their *Permanent Vacation* tour when their record company's marketing strategy called for further American dates. This left Guns N' Roses – and manager Alan Niven – with a high-risk dilemma. Should they wait to latch on to another big-

October 1987. Back in Britain. Balls out.

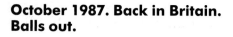

name British rock tour, or should they put their balls on the chopping block and headline their own set of dates? 'Balls out' being a way of life in Guns N' Roses, they headlined. Niven boldly booked the band into 2-3000-seat halls with only 10,000 sales of *Appetite For Destruction* to their name.

Guns N' Roses returned to Britain with the sweat still fresh from a brief US tour supporting The Cult. Axl comments: "Ian Astbury [The Cult's vocalist] came to our first show at the Marquee, the one we got such a slagging for, and liked it so much he offered us the tour! So fuck those journalists who wrote those bad things."

"Ian Astbury liked what he saw. We had a great time with The Cult. Ian spent more time in our dressing room than in his own!"

For their five UK shows, Guns N' Roses averaged ticket sales of 80 per cent of capacity. The final night at the Hammersmith Odeon fell just 200 tickets short of a sell-out.

As the band's fame escalated, so did their infamy. Axl began in earnest his habit of ripping hotel telephones out of walls. Though a neat way to rid himself of aggression, it meant that ordering meals via room service was a touch problematic. Holes in varying sizes appeared in the walls of the band's hotels. Room furniture was haphazardly re-arranged. TV repair companies boomed. Over-zealous fans came close to overturning the tour bus in the north of England.

Axl began in earnest his habit of ripping hotel telephones out of walls. Though a neat way to rid himself of aggression, it meant that ordering meals via room service was a touch problematic.

Todd Crew had roadied for Guns N' Roses for three years. Working with the band seemed to give him

something else to live for besides his heroin habit. However, back in June, Todd passed out drunk for the whole of the first Marquee show. By the time Guns N' Roses made their return to London, Todd had died from an overdose.

At Hammersmith an embittered Axl dedicated Dylan's 'Knockin' On Heaven's Door' (a song they had played for the first time in public at the Marquee) to Todd's memory.

If those five shows in October '87 lacked some of the mania of their British debut – where Slash and Duff stagedived into the Marquee crowd – they were still hard proof that Guns N' Roses' fireball charisma doesn't dissipate in bigger, colder arenas.

Having conquered as prestigious a venue as the Hammersmith Odeon, Guns N' Roses had, by the end of 1987, achieved a credibility and a status above that merited on their record sales alone.

While Aerosmith stayed rooted in their own backyard, Guns N' Roses dared and won.

Right and below: Axl on roadie Todd Crew's street-illegal hog in Los Angeles, where Todd overdosed and died.

"CAPTAIN AMERICA'S BEEN TORN APART..."

'Sweet Child O' Mine' melted the very heart of America. In the week of 10 September 1988, 'Sweet Child' became Guns N' Roses' first and (to date) only number 1 US single, helping transform *Appetite For Destruction* into one of the phenomena of 1980s rock 'n' roll.

By September of the next year, three more top 10 singles had been amassed: 'Paradise City', 'Welcome To The Jungle' and 'Patience'. Intense roadwork broke America when many predicted it would break Guns N' Roses.

"They didn't expect us to last a week!" snorts Izzy. "Touring really doesn't faze you. If you get twisted

backstage, the walk to the bus is only a few yards, y'know? But yeah, if you get twisted every night, you start draggin'."

"Touring has its downfalls," admits Slash. "It's a distorted kind of reality, but I swear to God, that 45 minutes or whatever makes it all worth it. When you're not touring you're always looking for something to fulfil that buzz."

"The thing about being on the road constantly is that you never really have any big problems hanging over you the whole time. When you're moving around from city to

"It's more addictive than any drug I could imagine," adds Izzy. "It's fucking terrible coming off the road. You come down real hard. It's like the world stops moving."

city you don't think about anything except getting to the next gig. Then when you come off the road this whole other world that's been waiting for you starts fuckin' with you. I mean, I hate having to deal with normal day-to-day shit. It leaves no time for anything else."

Guns N' Roses spent time at the beginning of 1988 headlining a tour of US theatres, but major arena supports offered great exposure. In November '87 they were invited on to Mötley Crüe's 'Girls, Girls, Girls' tour when Whitesnake quit to undertake headline shows of their own. Crüe plus Guns was hell on wheels.

Steven Adler broke a fist in a bar brawl and was replaced on a number of dates by Cinderella drummer Fred Coury, but the tour's major casualty was Crüe bass player Nikki Sixx. Sixx once lay clinically dead for a full two minutes as the result of a massive heroin overdose and was only saved by paramedics kickstarting his heart

Below: **Dallas. Axl exchanges his hat for one which Duff begged off photographer Ian T. Tilton.**

with shots of adrenalin. The Crüe's tour was cut short when Sixx retired "exhausted." Guns, meanwhile, raged on.

In May Guns N' Roses joined the start of Iron Maiden's North American tour in Canada but pulled out as the dates wound down the West Coast towards LA. Axl's voice was shot from too much of a good time on the road.

By 15 July, when Guns began supporting Aerosmith, Axl's self-discipline had strengthened. He denied himself booze and remained hidden away behind his hotel room door while Izzy, Slash, Steve and Duff blitzed every club and bar under the night stars. Axl would often appear just 20 minutes before a show and psyche himself up to a loud playback of Queensrÿche's 'The Needle Lies'.

Explains Slash: "You gotta understand that with this bunch, excess is best an' all that shit. Axl knows he has to keep from smoking or drinking or doing drugs to maintain his voice. He doesn't hang out that much because the atmosphere that's created by the other four members of this band is pretty, uh . . ."

"Conducive to deterioration," Izzy smiles.

"He just hangs out by himself. He takes it all pretty seriously. I couldn't do it," Slash confesses. "He's doing well to maintain a certain sanity level seeing as he can't go out 'cos of his position in the band. If he was doing what we were doing he wouldn't be able to sing at all!

"The Aerosmith tour was the first *rock 'n' roll* tour we've done. The Mötley tour was fun, but the vibe between us and Aerosmith was great.

"Those guys are around their 30s and 40s, they've been through a lotta shit and we have a lotta respect for them. We grew up listening to their music; this and the Stones and AC/DC, that's what sorta formed what we are. That's the only way you get any kinda personality – through influences."

On that tour, guitarist Joe Perry's Toxic Twins T-shirt was Aerosmith's only throwback to their mid-'70s chemical haze." Clean, detoxed, Aerosmith had hung up their wild years. Guns N' Roses' were only just beginning. . . .

On and offstage in Dallas. Tour manager, and now co-manager, Doug Goldstein blows a raspberry, sort of.

While Slash chugged bourbon between songs, Perry, a good 15 years his senior, swigged from a bottle of mineral water.

"It's funny," grins Slash. "They like to talk about drugs. They don't *do* drugs, they just like to talk about them, it's cool to be around that."

"You drag your ass into the gig sometimes," laughs Izzy, "and you

**Starplex Arena, Dallas, Texas.
24 July 1988.**

see those guys and you think, Awww, fuck!"

"They're eating watermelon and drinking tea," Slash continues, incredulous. "They love to ask you about what you did last night and how fucked up you got. They go, man, I've been up since nine o'clock this morning, and you say, What drugs are you doing? They say, No, I just been up since nine!

"When we got to LA it was a gas. We did 'Mama Kin' together. It was nice, too, because we were told by the people that worked for them that they would never go to the side of the stage and watch any of the bands that opened for them usually. But for us they were there just about every night. The first time I looked over and saw them all standing there watching us play, that fucked with me, it was weird.

"I did a guitar solo one night – one of those finger-pickin' slow blues things – and after the show, Steven Tyler [Aerosmith vocalist] got me to one side and said, 'That was amazing!' I just stood there and said, 'Well, thanks,' and couldn't think of anything else to say. I was blown away. That's something I'll never forget."

By September and the tour's end countless cigarettes and at least a fifth of Jack Daniel's per day had turned Slash's tongue a disgusting brown-black. Yet, incredibly, Guns N' Roses had survived their two-year

sex, drugs 'n' rock 'n' roll marathon. They even pulled through a crazy mid-tour crisis that left the band minus a singer for three days.

In February 1988 Axl didn't show up for a gig in Phoenix, Arizona. When he did appear the following day, the rest of the band, angered and disappointed, told Axl he was out of Guns N' Roses. The bitterness lasted for three tense days before Slash and Izzy met with Axl and heard out the singer's reasons for missing the Phoenix show. They quit bitchin' and made up, but the hurt lingers even now.

Above: Steven Tyler of Aerosmith. Dallas 1988. The Aerosmith/ Guns N' Roses American tour was dubbed The Greatest Rock 'N' Roll Double Bill ever seen.

"That's been one of the stories that's gotten bigger than all of us," sighs Slash. "And as little as it was, it's past tense and it's not worth talking about 'cos it doesn't relate to what's going on now."

Guns N' Roses do not swallow their pride too often, but on this one occasion, a little humility saved them.

By September and the tour's end countless cigarettes and at least a fifth of Jack Daniel's per day had turned Slash's tongue a disgusting brown-black.

Below: Steven runs up one hell of a tab in a Dallas beerhole. Matching him drink for drink is Dave 'Jr' Elefson of Megadeth.

DUFF McKAGAN

Duff McKagan isn't the quiet man of Guns N' Roses. Nor is he the wild one. He's more the tall cool one; a little crazy but dependable, fun but rarely hysterical.

Born Michael McKagan in Seattle, Washington, 5 February 1965, Duff "grew up surrounded by music. They always played the rock stations in my house when I was a kid."

Duff was the youngest of eight chidren, most of whom were involved with local bands at some stage. Even his father had a love of music, singing harmonies in a barbershop quartet. It was Duff's brother, Bruce, who introduced him to the bass guitar.

"When I was in eighth grade Bruce gave me lessons and I just got right into it."

Between ages 15 and 19 Duff drifted in and out of 31 Seattle bands, shifting from bass to drums and on to guitar.

"I started out as a bassist and then a local band spotted me fucking around on drums and asked me to join 'em."

Duff was even offered a gig with UK punk brats The Angelic Upstarts.

"The band came to the States years ago with a guy called Andy Thompson on drums, but he wasn't working out. Anyway, they crashed at the house of a friend of mine while they were in Seattle, so I got to know them. At the time I was playing drums, and out of the blue one day they called me from San Francisco, said they were looking for a new drummer and asked if I'd be interested.

"I rehearsed with 'em, but they wanted me to move to England and I was shit scared of making such a jump. I turned 'em down and stayed with the band I was with at the time. I thought I'd made a wise choice, but that group disappeared without trace."

Aged 21, Duff tired of the Seattle club treadmill and decided to try his luck in LA. Then a guitar player, he chose to revert to the bass to help stack the odds a little more in his favour.

"I had heard the stories about LA, where there were millions of guitar players, and I really didn't think I was good enough to be one of the top players. So in order to get my foot in the door, I decided to get a bass and a bass amp and go down to LA!"

Duff played in just two LA bands. The first was Road

Duff McKagan. The coolest head in Guns N' Roses.

Guns N' Roses vodka-swillin' token cowboy, on stage and in the dentist's chair.

Crew, where he first encountered Slash and Steven but walked out on them when gigs, and even rehearsals, dried up. The second was Guns N' Roses. . . .

Duff was the first member of Guns N' Roses to marry, in May of 1988. The band was already booked to play shows in Canada with Iron Maiden but the wedding received the official go ahead when a temporary replacement for Duff was found, namely Haggis, ex of The Cult and a friend of Guns N' Roses. They and Haggis had played on the same bill when the bassist was still a part of UK cock-rocker Zodiac Mindwarp's Love Reaction. Duff's bride was Mandy Brix, singer with LA band The Lame Flames.

"She's in a band," Duff winks, "so she understands life on the road."

As Izzy once remarked, "Duff loves his vodka" – the fifth bottle of Russian Stolichnaya on the band's backstage rider is his – yet he remains the most "even-keeled" of the five. He's the first one to pick up a football and fool around with the crew.

On tour, Duff works out each day with weights. In addition, he completes running exercises up flights of stairs. At home in Los Angeles, he has a mountain bike on which he covers 30 miles per day of hilly terrain.

"I've gotten into three fights recently with guys just trying to show off to their girlfriends. I won all of 'em, though," he grins. "I ride that bike constantly, so I'm in good shape."

This also helps Duff stand up to all that Stoli. He and Slash, Guns N' Roses' alcohol-poisoning club, checked into a Japanese hotel as 'The Likesheet Brothers – Phil and Luke.' When Duff mixes his guests a vodka and orange, he adds barely enough juice to colour the spirit, let alone flavour it.

Along with Slash, Duff handles around 90 per cent of publicity chores once the band's up and rolling on tour. And, at the end of a tour road-fever exacts its toll on Duff's appearance. There are few sights in rock 'n' roll to compare with Duff McKagan in a CBGB's vest, sweatpants cut off at the thigh, bare knees, snakeskin boots and a tacky stetson.

"This song," chokes Axl from a stage in Texas, "features Duff McKagan – our token cowboy – on bass."

The crowd, of course, loves him.

"I've gotten into three fights recently with guys just trying to show off to their girlfriends. I won all of 'em, though," he grins. "I ride that bike constantly, so I'm in good shape."

There are few sights in rock 'n' roll to compare with Duff McKagan in a CBGB's vest, sweatpants cut off at the thigh, bare knees, snakeskin boots and a tacky stetson.

Public Enemies at Number One

August 1988 was a bittersweet month for Guns N' Roses. When they arrived in England, via Concorde, for an appearance at the annual Monster Of Rock festival at Castle Donington, *Appetite For Destruction* had just hit the number one position in the US albums listings, ousting Tracy Chapman's eponymous debut.

Peaking 13 months after its release, *Appetite* was an unlikely number one; unapologetically loud, foul-mouthed and bloody-nosed, raw and glaring like a fresh tattoo burnt into tender new skin.

"I think the only reason it could possibly have gone to number one is because we're filling some sort of void," argues Slash. "It's not because the songs are all huge hits – that's the last thing they are. They're just a bunch of dirty rock 'n' roll songs. So I figure we're just the resident down-and-dirty rock band in town at the moment. Everybody wants to have that record because it's not really that safe . . . and it looks cool next to the George Michael records in their collection."

A number one record was perhaps the ultimate triumph of Guns N' Roses' integrity, but the euphoria wasn't to last. A huge crowd of 107,000 rock fans squeezed into the Donington site on August 30. Two never made it out alive. They were lost in the crush at the front of the stage, trampled and suffocated in Donington's thick red mud. Guns N' Roses were on stage as they died.

The Guns were unaware of the

"So I figure we're just the resident down-and-dirty rock band in town at the moment. Everybody wants to have that record because it's not really that safe . . . and it looks cool next to the George Michael records in their collection."

Opposite: Donington Park, August 1988.

Axl at Donington.

Donington 1988. Triumph before tragedy.

fatalities until they returned to their hotel in Leicester late in the afternoon. However, sensing panic and danger in the crowd (provoked by the collapse of a giant video screen at one side of the stage), they had attempted to calm the pushing, shoving mass with a concentration of slower songs. 'Patience' and 'Sweet Child O' Mine' ended their set. Axl left the stage with words that would take on a grim irony: "Don't kill yourselves."

"I don't know really what to think about it," Axl admitted later. "I don't want anybody to get hurt. We want the exact opposite."

"We didn't tell people to smash each other. We didn't tell people, 'Drink so much alcohol that you can't fucking stand up.' I don't feel responsible in those ways."

Slash adds: "When things started getting out of hand we had to stop the set to get those kids out of the crowd. We *had* to stop. I remember looking down into the crowd at the front of the stage thinking, 'Oh fuck!' When we were back at the hotel Alan [Niven] told me what had happened and I couldn't believe it. I've thought about it a lot since then, though, and I've decided I can't take personal responsibility for what happened at Donington. The way I see it, it was too many people pushing up to the stage.

"What really bums me out the most, though, the thing that really pisses me off, is the thought that somebody was standing on top of somebody else, and didn't care, or was too selfish or too self-involved to care. You can't stand on somebody and not know they're there. It's sick.

"There's been a couple of gigs where we've consciously had to slow down a gear. Donington, of course, was one of them. There was another gig, in upstate New York on the Aerosmith tour, which was particularly intense too. After we got off stage, the medics' booth outside was just loaded with kids."

Guns N' Roses have pushed crowds to the brink of chaos, but, as the Donington tragedies proved, the madness must end somewhere. In Saratoga Springs, New York, "there was nearly a riot," admits Izzy. "I get off on that kind of vibe, where anything's just about ready to crack. When there's 25,000 people and they have, like, three security guys. God, it was intense, man. It was just on that fucking edge of 25,000 people coming down on the stage."

"At times, like in Philly," reckons Axl, "I think I could've easily started a riot. It's great watching 'em go crazy but I don't want to see people get hurt."

"I'd been wondering whether we should write something to the parents of those kids who died at Donington," reveals Slash. "But then I thought that nothing which comes from us was gonna be that much of a statement to make to those people anyway. They don't want to read some shit from some simple-minded rock band who the parents haven't even heard of but were responsible, as far as they're concerned, for the demise of their children. So in the end I decided to leave it alone."

"I actually don't know if the acci-

> "At times, like in Philly," reckons Axl, "I think I could've easily started a riot. It's great watching 'em go crazy but I don't want to see people get hurt."

dent was our fault or not," shrugs Duff. "If someone were to ask me face-to-face whether Guns N' Roses were to blame, I couldn't say with any conviction that we're not. I don't think we can be held responsible, but maybe we have to take some of the blame. After all, we were on stage when those kids died, and had Guns N' Roses not existed then perhaps the tragedy wouldn't have occurred.

"It weighs very heavily on us and whatever anyone else may write or say about the incident can't make us feel any worse. Quite honestly, we couldn't give a fuck about the media trying to make us the scapegoats. That thing will haunt me forever anyway. It's strange, but tragedy and pain do seem to dog our career."

Slash displays his style at Donington.

"That thing will haunt me forever anyway. It's strange, but tragedy and pain do seem to dog our career."

"We don't go out of our way to look for trouble," insists Slash, "but the slightest incident takes on unbelievable proportions. We cause some chaos, because we think that's what rock 'n' roll is all about. Most groups are happy to do as they're told in order to be commercial and succeed, even give up their identity. We never wanted to do that.

"That's why we're the new public enemy number one, and every sheriff and cop wants just one thing, to nail one of Guns N' Roses."

"That's why we're the new public enemy number one, and every sheriff and cop wants just one thing, to nail one of Guns N' Roses."

Above: Security staff pull one fan to safety from the Donington crush.

Below: Slash backstage at Donington with Jeff Young (then of Megadeth), Lars Ulrich of Metallica and Dave Mustaine of Megadeth.

IZZY STRADLIN'

Where Axl possesses "a natural ability to attract attention, much of it negative", Izzy Stradlin' has the ability to be "invisible". Izzy can slip unnoticed from a room. Cool, languid, he's perhaps the most withdrawn of the five no-goods who make up Guns N' Roses and has experienced some difficulty in coming to terms with life as "a Beatle".

The other four band members have all bought properties with their royalty earnings. Izzy has spent comparatively little of his money. He's bought a car, but no home. Indecisive, living on his nerves, Izzy has hoarded.

He was born plain Jeff Isabelle in "Bumfuck" (read 'Lafayette'), Indiana, 8 April 1962.

"The fact that I'm from Indiana," he spits, "has no business being in my career! It's a worthless fucking place."

Izzy and Axl go back to their early teens. Izzy's always been cooler, quieter, though no less intense. Axl has the blacker police record but Izzy has survived the "toxic hell' of hardened drug addiction, just as Axl got out while he could. Though introverted, Izzy is resilient. In the words of Guns N' Roses old LA flyposters: 'Only the strong survive.'

As the only member of the band to graduate from college with a degree, Izzy can't be typecast as the untameable rock rebel illiterate. He's happiest with a bottle of Valpolicella and a Rolling Stones album. On Guns N' Roses' first visit to London in the summer of '87 he blew a bunch of per diems on a couple of Stones tapes, *Some Girls* and *Sticky Fingers*, which he required as inspiration right there and then.

Izzy has been likened to Keith Richards on many occasions. This is fine as regards great rhythm guitar playing, but isn't he concerned that this reckless rock 'n' roll life will leave him looking like Keef warmed up inside 15 years?

"I think Keith's held up pretty well!" Izzy laughs.

Duff, Slash and Steven generally like to hit the blacktop soon after a show and roll into the next town in good

As the only member of the band to graduate from college with a degree, Izzy can't be typecast as the untameable rock rebel illiterate. He's happiest with a bottle of Valpolicella and a Rolling Stones album.

Izzy relaxes with a guitar, a bottle and a girl.

Right: Soundcheck (left) and the show proper (right). Dallas 1988.

time for their day off. Travelling on a separate tourbus, Izzy and Axl prefer to linger, to go into the city and socialize.

Early press coverage created a different image of Izzy, depicting him as cheerless and acidic, Guns N' Roses' "resident cynic."

His brutal retorts ("What's the bullshit with the ages?", "Seattle? No-one's from Seattle", "Fuck you and your magazine!") were more than simple bloody-minded invective. Izzy demonstrated his impatience with dull questions by exploiting the sharp end of his dry humour.

He's not above toilet humour either. On one hot, lazy afternoon in America's South, Izzy couldn't get British photographer Ian Tilton into the tourbus shit-house quick enough. "Hey, Ian, get a load of this!" An emotional Izzy had just laid the longest turd of his life and made sure that the coiled monster was immortalized on film.

Izzy Stradlin' is the most independent of Guns N' Roses. All he asks of road manager (and now co-manager) Doug Goldstein is to be left to himself.

Privacy is sanity and Izzy will often just take off alone in a hired car. No girlfriend, just him and his thoughts.

"I don't think drugs or anything else is as important to anybody in that band as being in Guns N' Roses is," said country/rock singer Steve Earle, a friend of the band.

Earle's right. Izzy's still around.

W. Axl Rose Ate My Poodle

Shocking fans and critics alike, Guns N' Roses turned the 'new Aerosmith' mantle on its head with the release in November '88 of *GN'R Lies*.

Originally titled 'The Sex, The Drugs, The Violence: The Shocking Trust', *Lies* coupled *Live ?!*@ Like A Suicide* (re-released by public demand; secondhand copies of the initial pressing had been selling for more than $100) with four new cuts that owed more to the Rolling Stones than to Aerosmith.

The sleeve of *GN'R Lies* parodied the tabloid newspapers that had warned Britain of the imminent arrival of "dog-killing rockers" Guns N' Roses back in 1987. "The artwork," remarked Slash during his vodka binge of '88 (sick of 'Jack', he was sinking "around three litres of vodka per day"), "is a sorta *Sunday Sport* or *Sun* kinda vibe, with a Page Three girl on it. We did this EP for the same reason as we first did *Live ?!*@ Like A Suicide*. It's material that we wanted off our chests but without taking up too much space."

Commenting on the rough nature of the EP's mix, he added: "It's real simple, real sloppy. You can hear us talking, there's guitar picks dropping. Real off-the-cuff."

"Half-assed" Duff calls it, but the songs are great and the performances honest and electric. "Half-assed" or not, *GN'R Lies* joined *Appetite For Destruction* in the US top 10 in February of '89 and has sold in excess of two million copies in America alone.

'Patience' had been worked into shape on the Aerosmith dates and as a single made the charts in both Britain and the USA. Reminiscent of the Stones' 'Dead Flowers', 'Used To Love Her' is, says Izzy, "a joke. Wife beating's been around for 10 million years or something. I mean," he laughs, quoting American sledgehammer comedian Sam Kinison, "I don't advocate it. I *understand* it. But I don't treat women any differently than I treat men."

"If some guy goes out an' kills his girlfriend," says Slash, "that's gonna fuck my head up. I mean, this is serious. It's affecting the lives of people you don't even know, which is definitely a scary thing, to have that much power. The version of 'You're Crazy' is slow, mid-tempo, sorta half-time of what's on *Appetite*. It's a lot bluesier. That's the way me 'n' Axl 'n' Izzy originally wrote it, on an acoustic. Then we went into rehearsals for the album. I had a huge Marshall stack and my Les Paul and we

"If some guy goes out an' kills his girlfriend," says Slash, "that's gonna fuck my head up. I mean, this is serious."

just doubled it up right away and turned it into a real fast song."

It was 'One In A Million', however, which created the ugly controversy promised by *Lies'* tacky sleeve. Originally titled 'Police And Niggers', 'One In A Million' is a brutal recounting of Axl's early years in Hollywood. It isn't pretty.

"I went back and forth from Indiana eight times in my first year in Hollywood," Axl recalls. "I wrote that song about being dropped off at the bus station and everything that was going on. The black dudes trying to sell you drugs is where the line 'Police and niggers, get out of my way' comes from. I've seen these

1988. Trouble he
trouble the

huge black dudes pull Bowie knives on people for their boom boxes [ghetto blasters] and shit. It's ugly.

"When I say I'm a smalltown white boy I'm just saying I'm no better than anyone else I've described. I'm just trying to get through life, that's all."

'One In A Million' aims some low punches – "Immigrants and faggots, they make no sense to me/They come to our country, and think they'll do as they please" – but Slash reckons the outrage provoked by the song hinges on a single word.

"You have to watch this shit, you say. 'Police and niggers' was a line I really didn't want Axl to sing, but, y'know, Axl's the kind of person who will sing whatever it is he feels like singing. What that line was supposed to mean was 'niggers' in the sense of the sort of street thugs that you run into in LA. Especially if you're a Midwestern, naive young kid just coming into the city for the first time, and there's these guys trying to pawn this on you and push this on you. It's a heavily intimidating kind of thing for someone like that. I've been living in Hollywood so long, I'm used to it."

Yet while respecting Axl's right to freedom of expression, Slash can't help being disappointed that a "great track" has been spoilt, or at least overshadowed, by controversy.

"It bothers me because I'm part black and I don't have anything against black individuals at all. And what else bothers me is that one of the nice things about Guns N' Roses is that we've always been a people's band, and we've never really segregated our fans. And then with the release of that song, I think it did something that wasn't necessarily positive for the band. Personally, I don't think that statement should have been made. I talked to my mom – who lives in Europe – for the first time in ages and I asked her on the

> "And what else bothers me is that one of the nice things about Guns N' Roses is that we've always been a people's band, and we've never really segregated our fans."

phone if she'd heard the EP yet, and she told me no, right?

"But my little brother was out there with her, and when he came back he told me, yeah, she actually had heard it, but she was so shocked that we'd said something like that, she didn't know what to say to me about it."

"If we offended anyone," says Slash, "it wasn't intentional."

Ultimately, the controversy will cool and die and *GN'R Lies* will be regarded as great rock 'n' roll, pure and simple. Izzy and Alan Niven

believe it might have been greater still. They argued that the original sessions, cut in early '87, "kicked shit" out of the 1988 recordings. Axl, however, was unhappy with his performance from '87, so the latter tapes eventually made it into the record stores. One song from the lost *Lies* sessions, the lewd 'Corn Chucker' (just look at an ear of corn, they smile), may well surface on GN'R's projected X-rated EP (in addition, punk songs by Fear, Misfits, Sex Pistols and Adolescents are likely to constitute yet another EP).

"The *Lies* EP is another aspect of our abilities," says Axl. "We can only put so many songs on one album, and we wanted *Appetite For Destruction* to be a full hard rock record from beginning to end. The reason we released the EP was so that we don't get pigeonholed into one type of music that people expect from us. We like all kinds of music and we'll play all types of music.

> "When I say I'm a smalltown white boy I'm just saying I'm no better than anyone else I've described. I'm just trying to get through life, that's all."

> "We have pieces of everything in our band. You don't see a lot of that any more. Queen used to do it, and Zeppelin, but nowadays people tend to stay in one vein. Play whatever the fuck you want to play. That's what we've done."

"Don't Point Your Finger at Me"

Controversy sticks to Guns N' Roses like a shadow. 'One In A Million' was a storm in a thousand (ironically, it was the word "faggots" and not "niggers" which sparked a fury over the song and resulted in Guns N' Roses being banned from appearing at an AIDS benefit show in New York in the summer of '89).

It all began with horror tales of substance abuse. For early LA shows, Guns N' Roses' billing read 'fresh from detox'. Smack, sex, booze, tattoos – their craving for excess sucked on the '70s but reeked of danger.

When rock's newest miscreants made for London and the Marquee Club, British families locked up both their daughters and their dogs, lest these canine-killin' crazies felt the uncontrollable urge to rub out a few more little critters. In fact, Axl had merely joked about slaying poodles. He did shoot a pig in LA one night in 1989 with a single bullet between the eyes, but only for a barbecue.

British families locked up both their daughters and their dogs, lest these canine-killin' crazies felt the uncontrollable urge to rub out a few more little critters.

He did shoot a pig in LA one night in 1989 with a single bullet between the eyes, but only for a barbecue.

Backstage at the Starplex, Dallas, 1988. There are 15 minutes till showtime.

Further British public outcry greeted the release of *Appetite For Destruction* in its original sleeve; the Robert Williams painting depicted a robot which had raped a girl and now faced annihilation by some sabre-toothed vision from hell. A number of major retail chains – W.H. Smith among them – refused to stock the record until the cover was re-designed.

"I submitted the *Appetite* cover as a joke," says Axl, "'cause I didn't think anyone would use it. I just really liked it and tossed it in, and everybody else flipped! I couldn't believe they really wanted to use it."

Allegations of sadistic sexism were rejected by the band. Williams, they argued, was portraying the rape of its people by a savage society.

The lyrics of *Appetite* were branded "irresponsible". Slash comments on 'Mr Brownstone' and its discourse on heroin: "We never said it was cool, but if kids misunderstood it then that fucks me up. I don't want to be a part of fucking up kids' lives."

Radio wouldn't touch the first UK single. Peppered with obscenities, 'It's So Easy' was one of the great punk songs of the 1980s.

At Donington in '88, Guns N' Roses did all in their power to quell the chaos. They were blameless, but those two deaths put the band's comments on crowd violence into a cold new perspective.

Fistfights, riots, arrests, fines; controversy has raged at virtually every roadstop Guns N' Roses have made.

When they toured Australia in December of '88, the local authorities mistakenly felt that Axl's preamble to 'Mr Brownstone' condoned and glorified drug misuse; this was deemed a public offence and a warrant for Axl's arrest was issued. Police staked out the band's hotel but they had already hot-footed it to New

Zealand. Following their gig in Auckland, Guns N' Roses' home journey was re-routed to avoid Australia, where the police warrants were presumably still valid.

Trouble in Australia was fated: only three months before those dates, GN'R ran up a feud with those darlings of Australian rock, INXS. INXS were headlining a show at Dallas's huge Texas Stadium, with Guns N' Roses second on the bill.

By their own admission, Guns played a lousy show. They hadn't carried out a soundcheck.

As he left the stage, Axl upheld the great Texan ethic of 'biggest is best'; naturally enough, when INXS' name came up, the insulted flowed from there.

Slash and Axl: toxic twins.

Straight-talking, opinionated, Axl won't bite his lip, back off or sweeten his tongue. His are brutal words, but then, like Slayer or Metallica, Guns N' Roses are "a brutal band for brutal times."

WE'RE DOIN' WHAT WE WANNA AND WE'RE PULLING IT OFF

"Rock 'n' roll in general has just sucked a big fucking dick since the Pistols," snarls Izzy.

"I hope we've re-introduced the idea of being natural, of being for real and adopting a down-to-earth approach," says Slash. "We want to put integrity back into music. What this industry's about these days is pretty obvious – trying to polish everything up. Everything's like technopop, even heavy metal stuff.

"We go against every standard of this industry. Even when we play live – we're like a club band when we play to, like, 20,000 people. We do whatever we feel like doing."

"It's really weird having such success," adds Duff. "People tell me how great we are and I think to myself, 'We haven't done anything yet'! All this band has done so far is put out one LP and a half-assed mini-album. I often wonder if we deserve what's happened to us. Still, we did tour forever and certainly paid our dues."

Guns N' Roses kicked the shit out of the music industry. Only Tracy

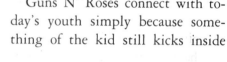

Guns N' Roses connect with today's youth simply because something of the kid still kicks inside

Chapman and Metallica have done likewise within the past decade.

Guns N' Roses reclaimed rock 'n' roll from the old and the weak. Their music draws on past eras but, hardened by a contemporary cynicism, the band don't cling to icons out of sentimental respect.

Izzy described a Rod Stewart show with a smile as "relaxing, like a quaalude." "I love Jimmy Page," sighed Slash while contemplating Page's LA Forum Show of 1988, "but he bores the fuck outta me sometimes!"

"Mick Jagger," he sneers, "should have died after *Some Girls*, when he was still cool."

them. On the Aerosmith trail in '88, tour manager Doug Goldstein went for an early morning round of golf on the course at the band's hotel and met with the sight of Duff, Slash and Steven – each huddled in his own motorised golf cart – racing the wrong way up the fairway and looking like rock's own Banana Splits!

What next for the definitive rock 'n' roll band of the age?

"We have a lot of stuff written," says Axl. "There are probably 30 songs to choose from already. We have about 10 ballads that I feel are more credible than 'Sweet Child O' Mine'."

'November Rain', which is eight minutes long, is among them.

"We wanted to save those ballads, because we wanted to wait until we had a bigger audience. We never imagined it would be this big, but we have some songs which we've been waiting to spring on people for a long time."

One off-the-wall number that is scheduled for inclusion on the new record is the rap song which Guns N' Roses played for two weeks on the Iron Maiden tour before Axl's voice gave in.

"Other than that, we're going to try and make the longest record that we can. We're going to try and put down as many songs as we can. I don't know if it will be a very, very long single album or maybe a double album."

"Rock 'n' roll is based on attitude," asserts Slash.

"We want to tour, travel, continue the big Guns N' Roses adventure," says Axl. "And indulge ourselves. And fuck a lot! Drug use is not in the past. We scare the shit out of each other because we don't want to lose what we have as a family."

> "This band is so realistic in what we do and what we play. We never said we were the best rock 'n' roll band in the world so don't judge us as that. We just go out and play."

It's Axl who has recently held Guns N' Roses together. The pressures of a hard and fast rock 'n' roll lifestyle had begun to tell as the band played four shows at the Los Angeles Coliseum as support to the re-

animated Rolling Stones. Early reports said that Axl had wigged out, that before the show he'd driven to the backstage area at the wheel of an LAPD squad car, siren wailing. And that he'd announced from the stage that he was quitting Guns N' Roses because too many of the band were "dancing with Mr Brownstone."

The last of these rumours bears the seed of truth. Axl was desperate to shake Slash, Izzy and Steven out of drugged stupors and felt the only way he'd do it was to threaten to quit the band. It worked.

On the second night Axl told the crowd there'd be no split. Slash said his piece on the perils of narcotics. He and Izzy and Steven cleaned up. Guns N' Roses survived.

"There *is* a self-destructive element about this band," concludes Slash, "but the will to survive is infinitely stronger – about twice as strong – and that will ensure we're gonna be around for some time to come."

The Best of Joe Weider's
MUSCLE & FITNESS
Bodybuilding Nutrition and Training Programs

Contemporary Books, Inc.
Chicago

Library of Congress Cataloging in Publication Data

Main entry under title:

The best of Joe Weider's *Muscle & Fitness:*
bodybuilding nutrition and training programs.

    1. Bodybuilding—Addresses, essays, lectures.
2. Nutrition—Addresses, essays, lectures.   I. Weider,
Joe.   II. Muscle & Fitness.
GV546.5.B47   1981   646.7'5   80-70631
ISBN 0-8092-5917-6   AACR2
ISBN 0-8092-5916-8 (pbk.)

All photos courtesy of the IFBB

Published by Contemporary Books, Inc.
180 North Michigan Avenue, Chicago, Illinois 60601
Manufactured in the United States of America
Library of Congress Catalog Card Number: 80-70631
International Standard Book Number: 0-8092-5917-6 (cloth)
                                           0-8092-5916-8 (paper)

Published simultaneously in Canada by
Beaverbooks, Ltd.
150 Lesmill Road
Don Mills, Ontario M3B 2T5
Canada

Contents

Everyone's a Winner in Bodybuilding

by Joe Weider

Americans have long believed that finishing first, being Number One spells success. But people now are realizing that this is not necessarily true. We have begun to define winning in new and personal ways. With the growing awareness of our physical beings we are becoming acquainted with a new kind of success that is not measured in medals or press clippings.

When we participate in any sport, we learn to accept our limitations and our assets. We learn about ourselves and our interactions with others. We are able to persist even when we lose. The benefits come from our investment in the training process, not the winning score. As we become firm, fit and strong, we find we are able to deal our private demons the coupe de grace and vanquish the dragons of stress, tension and misfortune.

The importance of victory for its own sake has become subject to reassessment. In fact, intense competition is a turn-off to a lot of people. Taken to a certain degree, competition can be healthy; taken to an extreme—victory at any cost—it can de destructive, defeating the basic purpose of the effort.

It's a healthy sign when 3000 people finish a marathon race. Entering and finishing can be far more permanent and satisfying than the fleeting glory of victory. Surely, Bill Rodgers must love to win marathon races, but his real joy comes from running the roads of Boston day to day. Otherwise, what would be the sense of him being in the sport in the first place?

In bodybuilding competition nobody understands the meaning of winning and losing better than Frank Zane. For three straight years he has worn the Mr. Olympia crown. Before that his competitive career had been a roller-coaster ride of ups and downs, the ups always falling short of his present position. Yet, he persisted. He never stopped training and trying. Contests became milestones. Frank has always made it clear that success for him has been the journey, never the destination. He is still traveling.

Today more people are treating sports as a regular, scheduled exercise routine to improve their health rather than to receive an award. The idea of group competition has always been important, especially for the young, because it teaches them sportsmanship and cooperation.

In the infinite variety available in bodybuilding, there is literally something for every body—health, fitness, improved appearance and a vibrant life-style, as typified by Frank Zane.

But sport for the sake of competition only is not the highest goal or purpose. Today we are finding that the true value of sports is the training that can offer a lifetime of mental and physical benefits.

Bodybuilding is an individual sport in which you can succeed on your own. Although the training experience can be shared with friends, there is no physical contact or mental tilting with a competitor. You become your own stiffest competition.

The need for recreation grows stronger in this success-oriented world of ours. We need time away from the stress of life. Bodybuilding teaches us how to relax. In an era of tension, skepticism and frustration, we can turn to bodybuilding for the simple, purifying pleasure of physical work. Bodybuilding can be an escape from "inescapable" tensions. It can literally save us from ourselves. It's one of the best things in life—and it's free!

Bodybuilding has become a special boon for women. The newfound freedom of women in today's society has introduced a whole new set of stresses into their lives. Sports in general and bodybuilding in particular are an excellent, healthy way to offset these stresses. In bodybuilding women have the opportunity to abandon the win-lose concept, and to enter a more challenging competition—that between their own physical limitations and mental discipline. Psychiatrists, therapists and endocrinologists prescribe sports to help inhibited women patients loosen up about sex. Getting in shape can condition you for an improved sex life and teach you how to handle your sexuality. Unlike men, women haven't traditionally been encouraged to use their leisure time for the enjoyment of athletics. Now they are experiencing what men have always known: they can get toned, better-looking bodies through a sports activity that's undertaken for the fun of it, not because it's a duty.

Nobody loses in bodybuilding. Both men and women, whether they train to compete or to get more enjoyment out of life, come out winners.

BODYBUILDING NUTRITION

The Balanced Diet

by Bill Dobbins and
Bernard A. Centrella

You don't have to be a biochemist to understand the basics of diet and nutrition. But an awful lot of bodybuilders seem to go out of their way to invite confusion. If you think there's no disagreement about how and what to eat to win bodybuilding contests, you should just listen to a group of bodybuilders discussing the subject.

"There's been a lot of progress in training techniques over the past 20 years or so," says Arnold Schwarzenegger. "But the real revolution has been in diet and nutrition."

Arnold himself is a good example. When he first arrived in this country in 1968, he had built his physique up to an imposing 250 pounds. But he felt he lacked something in the area of cuts and definition. So he set out to rectify this lack by making a study of diet and nutrition. When he combined hard training *and* sound nutrition, he achieved the physique quality to go with the mass.

No champion bodybuilder becomes a success without attention to the basics of training. Yet many fail to go as far as they might because they follow some dietary plan that ignores the basics of good nutrition. And if it's difficult for advanced bodybuilders who've been around long enough to know better, it's even worse for beginners and intermediates.

But learning to eat well is not that complicated. There are just three areas that require your attention:

1. *Nutrition*—What are the basic kinds of nutrients, and in which foods are they found?
2. *Diet*—What are the factors that result in weight gain or loss?
3. *Individual Differences*—How do these fundamentals apply to your own body type and metabolism? In what ways do you differ from the norm?

THE DEMANDS OF BODYBUILDING

The first thing to recognize is that bodybuilding is virtually unique in what it requires from an athlete. On the one hand, you are expected to create a highly unusual amount of muscle mass. This is done by strenuous, progressive-resistance exercise that tends, by its nature, to consume relatively few calories.

On the other hand, a competition bodybuilder is also expected to reduce the relative body fat content of the physique to abnormally low levels. Since bodybuilding training does not automatically result in burning up a lot of fat, this means that a strict, calorie-restrictive diet must be employed.

1

Most other athletes who need to develop a lot of strength (e.g., weightlifters, football players) don't have to rid themselves of anywhere near as much body fat as a bodybuilder. Athletes like gymnasts and marathon runners who engage in training that consumes a lot of calories rarely have weight problems. When your training burns up 5000–6000 calories a day, maintaining body weight rather than losing it becomes the problem.

Actually, surprising as it may seem, athletes in general don't have very good eating habits. They are, however, very concerned about nutrition and tend to be food faddists, always looking for a new gimmick or food supplement to give them an edge in performance. This often leads them to two erroneous conclusions:

1. To be better than my opponent, I must eat something different, something more exotic.
2. If a substance is good, more is better.

Again, a lot of them ignore the fundamentals of good nutrition; they tend to eat excessive calories and the wrong kinds of foods. The demands of their training burn up most of these calories. But once these athletes retire from competition and are no longer training hard, many of them have great difficulty adjusting their eating behavior to these new realities.

Bodybuilders simply can't afford a haphazard approach toward nutrition. If a diet provides too few nutrients and too many calories, it becomes immediately apparent when the competitor steps out onstage. When a football player lacks stamina, this may not become evident until the fourth quarter of a game. With the bodybuilder, any faults resulting from inadequate nutrition are obvious right from the start.

Bodybuilders need the same nutrients as anybody else. In some cases, they need more. The same fundamentals of balanced nutrition apply to the bodybuilder as to any other person or athlete. But these fundamentals have to be applied in a more disciplined manner. Therefore, it's important to the bodybuilder to have a more thorough knowledge of diet and nutrition, since he'll pay more dearly than most athletes for any errors.

BALANCING NUTRIENTS

The basic nutrients in food are:

1. Protein
2. Carbohydrate
3. Fats
4. Vitamins
5. Minerals

Balancing your intake of these nutrients is important because they interact with one another. The body, for example, requires some carbohydrate for the efficient metabolization of body fat. Also, many vitamins are able to work well in the body only in combination with other vitamins. In this sense, the basic nutrients act like members of an athletic team—if all members of the team don't pull together, individual excellence won't matter and the game will be lost.

After years of nutritional studies, the National Research Council recommends the following protein/carbohydrate/fat ratio for a balanced diet:

Protein	12%
Carbohydrate	58%
Fats	30%

The first thing about these recommendations that strikes the bodybuilder is the low percentage of protein. Athletes in general and bodybuilders in particular have always believed in large amounts of protein in their diet. To some degree, they're correct. When you're training very hard, and trying to build strength and muscle mass, you may very well need more protein than the average person.

But not all that much more. The average person needs about one gram of protein for every kilogram (2.2 lbs.) of body weight. The bodybuilder, on the other hand, should probably ingest one gram of protein for every two pounds of body weight—which comes out to 90 grams for a 180-pound man, or 100 grams for someone weighing 200 pounds.

Therefore, since bodybuilders are trying to reduce body fat far below normal, as well as increase muscle mass, they'd be advised to follow a diet with slightly more protein than recommended, and somewhat less fat—since fat contains such a large number of calories.

From our experience, to keep muscles actively growing, an average person should take 100 grams of protein in 3–4 meals—and never more than 30 grams per meal since the body cannot absorb more at one time. An active bodybuilder should get 150 grams of protein in 5–6 meals daily. Bodybuilders who have eaten less have experienced exhaustion, nervousness and loss of muscular size.

CARBOHYDRATE REQUIREMENTS

Carbohydrates come in two varieties: simple and complex. The two types act quite differently in the body. Simple carbs, like table sugar, enter the bloodstream very rapidly, cause insulin to be released for carbohydrate metabolization, and are eliminated rather rapidly.

Complex carbohydrates—the more biochemically complex forms found in vegetables—act more slowly upon the system (in an almost "timed-release" way) and provide a longer term source of energy for training.

Many people, some who should know better, use the word "carbohydrate" as if they were always talking about sugar. This is a mistake. While sugar is high in calories and provides nothing in the way of nutrition, carbohydrates found in vegetables provide valuable energy, vitamins and minerals, and must be included in a balanced eating plan.

The brain is powered solely by carbohydrate. When there is none in your body, your nervous system functions suffer. The minimum amount of carbohydrate it takes to keep these mechanisms going is 60–80 grams a day. Beyond that, additional carbs are necessary as an energy source for training. Therefore, individuals who go on an excessively low carbohydrate diet are hurting themselves in several ways:

1. They deprive themselves of vitamins and minerals.
2. They deprive themselves of energy.
3. They interfere with the body's ability to metabolize body fat.

The balanced diet should include some simple carbohydrate as well as the more complex kind. The latter should be in the form of lactose (from milk) and fructose (from fruit). Fructose, by the way, is many times sweeter than table sugar (sucrose) but occurs in nature in very small quantities. Due to its natural sweetness, fruit is often called nature's dessert.

INGESTION OF FAT

Fats, or oils, can be obtained from a variety of animal and vegetable sources. That marbled fat you see on steaks is only the most obvious kind. There is plenty more in the tissues, and in lots of other foods as well.

A certain amount of fat in the diet is natural, normal and healthy. But the ingestion of too much fat has been linked to problems like heart disease, and it puts an enormous number of extra calories into the diet. The calorie content comparison below shows why:

Protein	600 cal/lb
Carbohydrate	600 cal/lb
Fat	3500 cal/lb

If you're hiking in the wilderness, you might want to eat as much fat as possible because of its high energy value. But for a bodybuilder, extra fat—in the diet or on the body—spells trouble.

A lot of bodybuilders avoid meats like beef and pork because they're so high in fat; yet they eat an enormous number of eggs, which are loaded with it. True, eggs are probably the best source of protein, but an 80-calorie egg also provides you with six grams of fat. That's more fat than you get in 2½ ounces of lean beef. Eating 6–8 eggs a day, therefore, is not a good idea.

Whole milk is also high in fat—a cup provides nine grams. No wonder bodybuilders trying to get cut up avoid whole milk. Low-fat milk is not much better, since it has five grams of fat per cup. However, for those who like milk but still want to get as cut up as possible, there is nonfat milk, which contains virtually no fat at all.

Incidentally, a certain percentage of the adult population (higher among blacks, highest among

Orientals) lacks the enzyme necessary to digest milk. This is called "lactose intolerance." If you're one of these, don't fight it; avoid milk entirely.

VITAMINS AND MINERALS

Vitamins are organic nutrients; minerals are inorganic. These nutrients act as catalysts—they trigger other reactions in the body. To do the job, they need be present only in small quantities. If any are missing, however, the effect on the body can be quite devastating.

Here is a list of some of the Recommended Daily Allowances of the various vitamins and minerals:

Vitamin A—5000 IU
Vitamin C—60 mg
Vitamin B$_1$—1.5 mg
         B$_2$—1.7 mg
         B$_6$—2 mg
         B$_{12}$—6 mcg
Niacin—20 mg
Folacin—400 mcg
Pantothenic Acid—10 mg
Biotin—300 mcg
Vitamin D—400 IU
Vitamin E—30 IU
Calcium—1200 mg
Phosphorous—1000 mg
Iron—Males 10 mg
      Females 18 mg
Iodine—150 mcg
Magnesium—400 mg
Zinc—15 mg
Copper—2 mg
Linoleic Acid—About 1 tsp.
   vegetable oil (polyunsaturated)

Notice that for the most part we're talking about milligrams—$\frac{1}{1000}$ of a gram—when dealing with necessary amounts. Usually, a well-balanced diet containing a variety of foods provides the vitamins and minerals we need. However, a bodybuilder cannot afford to be lacking in *any* of the essential nutrients because a deficiency could interfere with training and cost him a title. Therefore, many bodybuilders wisely choose to take out some insurance as follows:

1. By ingesting a reasonable amount of vitamin and mineral supplements each day.
2. By consulting a qualified doctor to determine whether any deficiency exists.

Supplements are just insurance; they shouldn't be your major source of vitamins and minerals. True, during a period of particularly strict dieting, you may not be getting enough nutrients, and supplements become essential. But that should happen only occasionally. Remember, the only vitamins and minerals for which we have RDAs (recommended daily allowances) are the ones which are presently known. Who knows what other important nutrients in food have yet to be isolated?

As to medical tests, there are a number of ways of determining vitamin or mineral deficiency. For instance, a piece of your hair can be tested to measure the mineral content of your body. If you have been having trouble getting up for training psychologically, perhaps some deficiency is to blame. For the serious bodybuilder, occasional examinations are a valuable way of making sure you're at your best.

VITAMIN OVERDOSE

There are two kinds of vitamins—the water-soluble type, and those soluble in fat. This makes a difference in determining dosage.

Water soluble vitamins do not accumulate in the body. When you ingest more of these vitamins than the body can handle, the excess is simply flushed from the body in the excreted urine. (This also means that if you're taking water-soluble vitamins, it's better to take them several times a day in smaller doses, or to use the sustained-release type.)

Fat-soluble vitamins, on the other hand, are stored in the body and excess doses can build up to toxic levels. Overdosing on these vitamins can be dangerous.

As stated earlier, vitamins, minerals and other nutrients work in combination with one another. Hence, it's necessary to have a sufficient level of all of these nutrients. But once you have enough, additional amounts don't seem to do any good. Bodybuilders may well require more nutrients than the average person, but this means a little more of everything, not just one selected vitamin or mineral.

If you read, therefore, that the B-complex vitamins are required for energy production, this doesn't mean that taking additional doses will give you more energy. It only means that you can't produce energy in their absence. Excess vitamins and minerals don't help you any more than does additional protein. Take supplements to be safe, but when it comes right down to it, enough is enough.

THE BASIC FOOD GROUPS

There are various ways of dividing foods into the basic groups. One of the most traditional is:

1. Meat, milk and eggs
2. Fruits and vegetables
3. Grains and cereals
4. Legumes

The key to really balanced nutrition, and the reason for setting up the food groups in the first place, is variety. If you eat a little of everything, your nutritional needs get taken care of naturally.

You receive most of your protein from the first group, but there is also protein in vegetables, nuts, cereals, grains and seeds. Fruit has no protein but supplies a lot of valuable vitamins and minerals. There is such a variety of vegetables, of course, that you can go strictly vegetarian in your eating habits and still have a balanced diet.

In an attempt to lose as much body fat as possible, many bodybuilders restrict their diet so much that it fails to meet their basic nutritional needs. If you do this for a very short time, you can make up the deficiency with supplements. But over the long haul, your health and your physique will suffer if you deprive yourself of a sufficient variety of foods.

FOOD AND APPETITE

Hunger and appetite are two different things. Hunger is the need for food, appetite the desire to eat. Too often they're not very well-coordinated.

What we eat plays a part in balancing hunger and appetite. For example, when you eat carbohydrate, especially simple carbs, the sugar gets into your bloodstream quickly and satisfies your appetite. But this satisfaction does not last. Eating fat, on the other hand, does not satisfy the appetite quite so fast, but when satisfaction does come it lasts a long time.

The secret, therefore, is to eat a little of everything: carbs for immediate satisfaction, fats to take over when the carbohydrate is metabolized, and a wide variety of other foods to satisfy nutritional needs.

WEIGHT CONTROL AND CALORIES

Once you have achieved a fairly balanced diet, the next question is, how much to eat. The equation that applies here is easy to understand but somewhat more difficult to put into practice: eat more than you need and you get fat, eat less and you get lean.

In addition to its functions in building and maintaining the body, food is also energy. That energy is measured in calories, which are units of heat.

For the sake of survival, evolution has given us the capacity to store up energy for later use. We do this in several ways:

1. As glycogen in the muscles and the liver (carbohydrate energy).
2. As muscle tissue (the protein can be converted into energy).
3. As fat.

Glycogen reserves in the body are somewhat limited. In the absence of carbohydrate, the body can metabolize muscle tissue, but this is unhealthy and inefficient. The most natural and efficient method of storing and retrieving energy, therefore, is in the form of fat.

Remember, we said that a pound of protein represents 600 calories of energy, while a pound of fat is 3500 calories. This means body fat is a very efficient way of storing energy for later use, and 3500 becomes a fundamental number to plug into our equation. For every 3500 calories of food you eat in excess of body needs, the body creates one pound of fat; for every 3500 calories of energy you expend without enough food to provide the fuel, your body burns up one pound of fat.

Depending on your body weight and individual metabolism, every action in your life is fueled by a given number of calories. Here is the "caloric cost" of various activities:

Sitting	72–84 cal/hr.
Walking	240–300
Calisthenics	300–360
Jogging	420–480
Running	600–660

The heavier you are, the more calories you burn in moving your body around. The better your conditioning, the more intensely you can exercise and the more energy you use. A college football player may expend more than 5000 calories during a hard day's training. But on a rest day that same individual will probably burn up only half that amount.

Counting calories is difficult. Studies have been done in which individuals spent days in

sealed boxes and every single calorie of heat that came off their bodies was measured. But the actual influences on individual caloric consumption—outside temperature, clothing, hours of sleep, state of health, state of condition, etc.—are so complex that it's impossible to accurately determine how many calories any individual needs to gain, maintain or lose weight.

You can make guesses, and these serve as starting points. You might say, for example, that the average 150-pound man who is moderately active will need about 2600 calories a day. However, a muscular bodybuilder weighing 190 pounds may require 3500 calories to maintain that weight. But these are just guidelines. Another process is necessary to make closer determinations.

HOW MANY CALORIES DO YOU NEED?

While it's difficult to measure how much energy you are expending, you can get a good idea of how many calories you're ingesting.

There are numerous published tables that give caloric values for various foods. If you measure the amount of food you're eating, and look up the caloric values in these tables, you can get a pretty good idea of your caloric intake.

After this, it's merely a matter of trial and error. Suppose you record (in a notebook) the values of everything you have eaten for a week. You find that your daily average was 2100 calories and your weight loss for that week was one pound. You can then estimate that you have been functioning at a caloric deficit of 500 calories per day (7 × 500 = 3500 = 1 lb.).

There are other variables, of course. Water retention, for example. But keeping a calorie diary gives you some sort of picture of your eating behavior, and therefore you have somewhere to start when you introduce changes.

The other variable, of course, is exercise. Obviously, you burn up more calories when you're weight training than when you're taking it easy. If you're running and riding a bicycle in addition to training with weights, you'll use even more energy and metabolize additional fat.

When you train with heavy weights, you don't actually burn up that many calories. That's because the exercise is too intense to be continued for very long. But activities such as walking and running (where you move your own body weight around) can be carried on for long periods of time, and they burn up about 100 calories per mile. When making entries in your food diary on your caloric intake, you must also include some notation on the type and duration of exercise you did each day.

Of course, bodybuilders getting ready for a contest try to reduce their body fat to the barest minimum. Ordinarily, you're considered lean if you can pinch no more than an inch of fat in the abdominal area. For bodybuilding competition, obviously, more weight loss is necessary.

To achieve that additional weight loss you must:

1. Cut down on food intake, but maintain a balanced diet.
2. Increase your exercise.

Whenever you want to gain or lose weight, you should make the adjustment in all areas of nutrition so that you continue to eat a balanced diet. If you don't, especially when you're trying to lose weight, you'll interfere with the body's ability to produce energy—and, therefore, to burn fat.

Take the "zero-carb" diet, for example. Lots of bodybuilders have eaten nothing but tuna fish and water for weeks on end in an attempt to get cut up. But this produces a state called "ketosis," in which fat cannot be metabolized efficiently and the body begins to attack muscle tissue for additional energy and nutrition. In other words, the body in this state is not losing fat very fast and, to make matters worse, it's losing muscle mass. Does this sound like a good diet for contest preparation?

Eating too little robs you of energy and makes it hard to train. Training burns up energy and fat. If you train with less intensity, you burn less fat. So it stands to reason that too strict a diet is self-defeating.

What is called for instead is the right combination of exercise and diet. Every mile you walk or run means that you can take in 100 more calories and still lose the same amount of weight. In that 100 calories are the nutrients you need to help you get good workouts and, therefore, burn more calories.

As they get close to a contest, many bodybuilders do more sets and reps for definition. Okay, that does burn up more calories, but we have already pointed out that weight training is not particularly suited to burning a lot of calories. It would make more sense to stay with an intense workout in the gym, then go out and run, hike or ride a bicycle. The only restriction on outside exercise is that it

should not be so strenuous that it interferes with your gym workouts.

INDIVIDUAL DIFFERENCES

All the above guidelines, the figures (such as "3500 calories in a pound of fat") and the values for the amount of calories burned by exercise may convey the impression that everybody is alike. Well, everybody isn't.

First of all, there are different body types. Some people are naturally slim, others naturally muscular, while still others tend to be fat from birth. In all cases, the caloric content of the food consumed is the same; it's the individual metabolisms that differ.

This means that the rules for a balanced diet have to be applied with a little imagination. Certainly, the body is adaptable enough so that if you eat 20% protein instead of 12%, it can handle the difference. A bodybuilder, however, is not interested in getting by, but in getting to the top. He's seeking perfection.

Champion bodybuilders don't train alike, and there's no reason to assume they should eat alike. On a biochemical level, they all have to accomplish the same things, which means eating a balanced diet. But they may go about it differently. There are a number of variables.

1. *When to eat*—For years everyone was told, "Don't eat before going to bed." Recent studies, however, indicate it doesn't matter when you eat—the body handles it all the same way. So the question becomes when do you want to eat? What is most comfortable for you? Skip breakfast, eat four meals a day, five, eat early, late? The only rule is this: don't eat too much at once. The body can only metabolize food in certain quantities. Eating smaller meals more often is better than having big meals less often.

2. *What to eat*—You must have a source of each nutrient. But there are numerous sources. If you don't like cooked vegetables, try some that can be eaten raw in a salad. Can't drink milk? Try low-fat cottage cheese. But remember, a "good" diet isn't good unless the food is tasty enough so that you'll actually continue to stay on the diet.

3. *How much to eat*—Once you have satisfied your nutritional requirements, the rest of the food consumed is just excess calories. If you feel you lack energy, add some carbohydrate to your diet. Feel hungry all the time? Maybe some eggs or beef will provide the fat needed to satisfy that hunger. If you want to eat more meals a day, but fitting them in is difficult (you're in school, at work, etc.), try filling a thermos with a protein drink, perhaps with some fruit mixed in. But remember, count those calories, too.

GAINING WEIGHT

Many younger bodybuilders are interested in gaining rather than losing weight. Mostly, what they want is to acquire the kind of muscle mass that they see in their idols, the champion bodybuilders. Unfortunately, they don't want to wait for the mass to accumulate through exercise.

So they resort to a weight-gain diet, and this in itself is not a bad thing. A youth carrying only 6% body fat can afford quite a bit more weight (including fat) and still be healthy. Taking some sort of weight-gain supplement is a better way to do this than habitually overeating, a habit that will eventually become hard to break.

As you get older, your metabolism slows. Therefore, even if you're skinny now, your body will tend to put on weight later. So don't think of your condition as permanent.

And differentiate between muscle mass and body-fat weight. The bodybuilders you see in *Muscle & Fitness* have very little fat on them. That mass is all muscle, and some of them have worked as long as 20 years to build that kind of physique. If you want to gain some weight to look better while you're building muscle, just keep in mind that someday you might want to lose all that weight.

But the main thing is not to resort to an unbalanced diet in order to achieve the weight gain. Don't eat three quarts of ice cream. Eat additional meals, including high-calorie food and fruits, and supplement your diet with a weight-gain drink. Remember that long-term health and physical development will best be achieved by providing your body with the full range of nutrients it requires.

FOOD MYTHS

Many athletes and bodybuilders, as well as other individuals concerned about nutrition and weight control, do not take full advantage of the range of foods available in the various food groups. That's because they've been told certain things are fattening when they're not.

A good example is the potato. A medium potato weighing about ⅓ pound contains only 90 calories or so. It also contains three grams of

protein, nine grams of calcium and 20 mg of ascorbic acid (one-third that found in an orange). The potato provides a lot of bulk with very few calories, and it makes a great addition to a weight control diet . . .

Until you begin to add the butter (1 tablespoon = 100 calories), or the sour cream (1 cup = 485 calories). This is true of a number of foods. They're not to blame; it's what we add to them that causes the problem.

If you like a certain food, look it up in the caloric index and find out if it fits into your diet. Then be careful what you do to the food. A low-calorie but nutritious salad can become very fattening by the addition of a lot of salad oil at 100 calories per tablespoon. And a small pancake to go with your egg in the morning provides only 60 calories—until you load it with butter and syrup.

Knowing what you can eat is often just as important as knowing what you shouldn't.

THE BALANCED DIET—A SUMMATION

For quick reference, here's a handy guide to planning your own version of a balanced diet:

1. Include at least one gram of protein for every two pounds of body weight.
2. Ingest at least 60–80 grams of carbohydrate (you should take more if you're training hard).
3. Carbohydrate intake should be 75% complex–25% simple.
4. Fats should be limited to 30% or less of the total intake.
5. For more energy, increase your carbohydrate intake.
6. Vitamin and mineral supplements should be insurance, rather than the main source of these nutrients.
7. Eat from all of the major food groups: meat, fish and eggs; dairy products; vegetables and fruits; cereals and grains; legumes.
8. To lose fat, increase your exercise and moderate your diet without going below basic nutritional requirements.
9. Try not to use sugar or table salt.
10. Eat small meals more often rather than big meals less often.

THE LONG-TERM BALANCE

We would like to emphasize that these are just guidelines, not the Ten Commandments. Your own personal nutritional needs may very well differ from the norm, and you'll have to be prepared to make adjustments.

Another important point is that the body is very adaptable. It doesn't add up the accounts at the end of each day. If you get too little of something one day and a bit too much the next, the body is capable of balancing things out. You don't have to approach nutrition with a slide rule.

But you do have to get used to keeping track of what you eat. Without writing it all down, at least some of the time, it's easy to forget what and how much you ate. Once you have done this for a while, you may get to understand your own patterns so well that you'll have no need to continue keeping a food diary. But many advanced bodybuilders, even after getting to the top, continue to keep a careful record of what and how much they eat—just as they write down exactly what they do in the gym each and every workout.

A balanced diet is necessary to sustain the efforts it takes to become a champion. How you go about achieving that balance is an individual matter.

Carbohydrates:
Friend or Foe?

by Dr. Franco Columbu

Human nutrition and the physiology of energy production are highly complex and technical matters. But everybody seems to have an opinion on the subject anyway. Go to any gym in the country—probably in the world—and you'll hear bodybuilders delivering a constant flow of conflicting opinions on training diets, how to really get cut up, or how to produce the biggest gains in muscle mass. It can make your head spin.

The problem is, the opinions aren't backed up by any amount of study in nutrition and the metabolic process. They're based to some degree on experience or on hearsay. But there are so many factors involved that it's hard to decide which variations are really making the difference when you experiment with your diet.

In fact, the body tends to be so resilient that you can abuse it for some time without seeing any signs of damage. In other words, your "great diet discovery" may be the worst thing you've ever done to yourself, but you won't find out until after it's too late.

One of the most persistent myths in bodybuilding is that carbohydrates are bad. "I'm cutting back on the carbs to get really ripped" is a typical approach to contest preparation. Or it was. Nowadays, an increasing number of top contenders are changing their minds about carbs.

The idea that carbohydrates make you fat has gone hand in hand with the notion that more and more protein gives you bigger and bigger muscles. This is another example of the "something for nothing" school of thought. Bodybuilders following this theory cut down on their carbohydrate intake drastically and consume thousands of extra calories of protein under the illusion that protein calories automatically produce muscle, while carbohydrate calories inevitably turn to fat. This does not happen to be the case, however.

To really gain an understanding of the role of carbohydrates in the human metabolism—how they act to produce energy and interact with protein and fat—it might be a good idea to take a closer look at them.

To begin with, carbohydrates are simply compounds containing carbon, hydrogen and oxygen, with the hydrogen and oxygen in the same proportion as in water—you know, good old H_2O. The formula for carbohydrates, in case anyone should ask, is CnH_2nOn. Most carbohydrates are of plant origin, except for glycogen, lactose and ribose. Plants use carbon dioxide, water and sunlight in photosynthesis to produce carbohydrates, which are the major energy source of the animal kingdom.

Okay, so that's what carbs are. But what do they do? For the most part, carbs provide the

readiest source of energy for a variety of metabolic tasks, including muscular contraction. The body converts carbohydrates to glucose which the liver releases into the bloodstream as a means of fueling physical processes. Any excess is converted into glycogen, which is the way the body stores carbs. The glycogen can be changed back into glucose when you begin to run short of glucose in the bloodstream.

The liver is the main organ for synthesizing glycogen from glucose, but it's not the only one. The muscles of the body themselves—the skeletal, cardiac, and smooth muscles—also maintain glycogen stores, as do practically all the organs of the body (in small amounts).

When you first begin to use your muscles in a workout, you get energy from the oxidation of glucose and, to some extent, fatty acids. As you continue to exercise heavily, reserves of stored glycogen will be converted to glucose for additional fuel until that storage capacity is gradually eliminated.

When you take in more carbohydrates than your body needs for its supply of glucose, and more than it can store as glycogen, the excess calories are converted into fat and transported to the adipose cells. This, naturally, is what concerns bodybuilders. Adipose tissue is the mortal enemy of the competition bodybuilder.

But it's also true that *any* excess calories—carbohydrate, protein or fat—ultimately end up as stored body fat. So it makes sense to limit your overall caloric intake if you're trying to burn up fat stores, rather than merely to limit your carb intake. You must make your body dip into its stored energy—fat—and this means ingesting fewer calories than you burn. Period.

But there's another reason to keep carbohydrates in your diet. Carbs are "protein sparing." What this means simply is that the body, in the absence of sufficient carbohydrate, is forced to convert some of the protein you eat into energy, when that protein should really be used for tissue building and maintenance. While protein is great for building muscle, it's a lousy source of energy. A pound of protein yields only 600 calories, compared to the 3500 calories in a pound of fat.

When you have sufficient carbohydrate in your body, the protein you need for building muscle is not wasted. It has also been shown that you get the maximum protein-sparing action when carbohydrates and protein are ingested at the same time. This relates to that old dictum about

Dr. Franco Columbu

the necessity of eating balanced meals. Now we know why.

Another strong argument for including sufficient carbohydrate in the diet is that the brain relies almost exclusively on carbohydrates for energy. Have you ever noticed how forgetful, confused and irritable bodybuilders can get on a low-carb or zero-carb diet? They're actually interfering with the function of their brain and nervous system, which is hardly a good idea.

Severe carbohydrate deprivation leads to a state known as "ketosis." Many dieters have actually induced such a state on purpose because it does result in a lowering of appetite and in a rapid initial weight loss due to dehydration. But the diet also results in a depletion of lean body weight and, in some cases, even cardiac muscle. Modern sports nutritionists frown heavily on this approach to weight loss.

Okay, accepting the fact that carbohydrates are necessary and beneficial, the question remains: what foods are the best sources of this nutrient? Most vegetables, fruits and whole grains contain large amounts of carbohydrate. Fructose, the carbohydrate in fruit, is actually 50% sweeter than refined sugar.

When you eat a variety of vegetables—everything from broccoli to asparagus to beans—you're assured of a full complement of vitamins and minerals, as well as the carbohydrate your body needs. And, as any vegetarian will tell you, you can get a great deal of low-fat protein as well.

These vegetables also contain a lot of fiber, necessary to good operation of the digestive tract, and their relative bulk means you'll feel full on fewer calories.

What you must avoid is the refined variety of carbohydrate—candy, pastry, syrups, soft drinks and the like. These are "empty calorie" foods which contain relatively high calories and little or no nutritional value.

Of course, you must remember that too many calories, whether carbohydrate or not, will result in the production of fat. So the question becomes: how much carbohydrate is enough? For basic metabolic needs, such as brain function, you need something like 60–80 grams a day. In addition, you'll need enough to provide the glucose you require for fueling muscular contraction.

Whenever you exercise, you tend to burn some glucose and fatty acids. The proportion can vary tremendously depending on the kind of exercise you're doing. All physical energy comes from oxidation. When foods are oxidized in the body, carbon dioxide, water and heat are produced in direct proportion to the quantity of oxygen consumed in the process. Fats contain less oxygen in their molecules than carbohydrates do, so they need more oxygen from the atmosphere.

Carbohydrates are able to create energy in the absence of respiratory oxygen (remember the "O" in the carb formula?). This is called "anaerobic metabolism." Metabolism of fats using oxygen in the bloodstream is called "aerobic metabolism." In practical terms, what this means is that the kind of exercise which makes you breathe hard—constant, high-repetition movement—generally requires a great deal of endurance and burns primarily fatty acids. Short burst of activity, like lifting a heavy barbell a few times, is fueled for the most part by the oxidation of glucose—from carbohydrate.

In other words, a great deal of bodybuilding training burns up carbohydrate energy rather than fat energy. So a diet deficient in carbs is likely to severely restrict a bodybuilder's activities in the gym. Added to the 60 or so

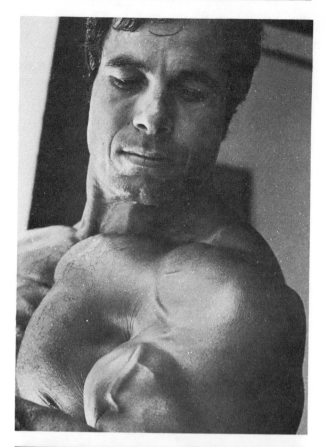

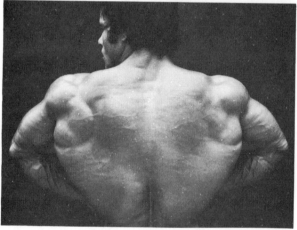

grams of carbohydrate that the body needs for the function of the nervous system, one needs another several hundred calories for physical exercise.

The reverse is true also. In order to get cut up, it makes sense to indulge in some exercise that requires endurance and high-repetition movement. Running, cycling, swimming and the like not only burn up a lot of calories but, compared to weight training, they also burn a greater ratio of fatty acids to glucose.

But the most important thing is to eat a properly balanced diet, with the correct proportion of carbohydrates to protein to fats, then to keep careful track of your caloric intake.

The current consensus as to what constitutes a balanced diet for a bodybuilder is:

FAT   25%
PROTEIN   20%
CARBS   55%

To sum up, carbohydrate deprivation is as serious a problem as eating too little protein, or not getting enough vitamins or minerals. Carbs constitute an essential food element. Without them, the healthy functioning of the body is impossible.

Since bodybuilders are interested in not just a healthy functioning body but a *superior* functioning body, they should be even more aware of the importance of this vital nutrient.

Bill Pearl Talks Vegetarian Bodybuilding

*by Bill Pearl
as told to Bill Reynolds*

Traditionally, bodybuilders have been the most carnivorous of carnivores. As often as six times per day, superstars and would-be-stars stuffed themselves with beef—from three to 10 pounds daily—to build massive muscles. The idea was to consume 300–400 grams of protein each day in order to give the muscles enough amino acids for maximum growth. Four-time Mr. Universe Bill Pearl thinks this procedure is a bunch of, uh, bull.

"A growing bodybuilder simply doesn't need 300–400 grams of protein to reach his potential," Pearl states emphatically. "If the protein is from a natural source and is cooked as little as possible, the human body can survive very comfortably—even grow—on only 50–70 grams per day. Furthermore, this protein does not need to be meat, poultry or fish, but can be from vegetable or dairy foods. Beef is actually fairly low in protein, because once you remove all the fiber, water and uric acid from a prime steak, very little protein remains.

"If a bodybuilder is eating 300–400 grams of protein per day and is cutting his calories in view of a contest, he's bound to become tired and lethargic. As a result, the body must take protein and try to convert it to blood sugar to train—a long process that consumes almost as much energy as it produces. If the bodybuilder doesn't have enough energy to train, why take in so much protein?

"The bodybuilder I'm discussing would be better off ingesting half or one-quarter of the protein he's eating, replacing the deleted meat calories with carbohydrate foods for energy. Carbohydrates are the body's preferred source of energy fuel, and anyone who eats an adequate supply of fresh fruit will have an abundance of training energy.

"There is absolutely no question that it is possible to build a high-class physique and be a vegetarian at the same time. A prime example is Roy Hillgen, a former Mr. America who is now 54 years of age, and who made a great impression on the judges at a recent Mr. International contest. Roy's been a vegetarian as long as I've known him, and I met the guy about 1949 or 1950.

"Steve Reeves was about as close to being a vegetarian as anyone I have known, and he's one of the most revered athletes in bodybuilding history. Steve was almost exclusively lacto-vegetarian and he ate only minor amounts of meat. During the times I've eaten out with him, Reeves was always eating salads, avocados, fresh fruits, fresh vegetables, plus some occasional milk products.

"I've personally been a strict lacto-vegetarian

Bill Pearl and Ben Weider

since 1971, and a semi-vegetarian since about 1963 or 1964. Back in the '60s, I was working with the astronauts and company executives at North American Rockwell. I was telling these people all about good health. We were taking treadmill tests, and I was knocking these guys dead.

"One day—just as a lark—the doctor checked my cholesterol. It was 307, an unbelievably high level, so my blood was running almost as thick as syrup through my veins. The doctor said, 'I don't give a damn how good you look, Bill, or how big your arm is. You're asking for trouble!' He went on to tell me I could die just as easily at 50 as anyone else if I continued the path I was following. Naturally, that started me thinking.

"Because of bodybuilding, I was somewhat afraid to stop eating meats, but after the doctor had told me this and I had competed in the 1967 Mr. Universe, I decided to change my eating habits. Becoming a lacto-vegetarian was my response to the situation, and except for a short period of meat eating before the '71 Universe, I've been a vegetarian since 1967. In 1971 I just wasn't convinced I could do it again without meat, but last year I got into shape for exhibitions at the American and Olympia on a strict lacto-vegetarian diet. Still, last year I weighed over 240 with good muscularity.

"Vegetarian eating has had numerous positive effects on my body. My cholesterol gradually dropped down to a normal level of 198, and the blood pressure lowered. My pulse rate and other physiological processes are much better, and overall I'm in better shape than I was 15 years ago.

"One of the most dramatic changes has been in my uric acid levels. My uric acid is now down to zero, but before it was so sky high that every joint in my body ached. My uric acid was once so high that I could hardly move my hands. I actually thought I was getting arthritis!

"Now my energy levels are incredible, and I feel like a million dollars all of the time. My 33rd year of training starts in August, and I definitely feel as good today as I did 30 years ago. There's nobody in my club, or anyone I've ever trained with, that I couldn't stay up with in a hard workout. My energy is greater than ever, and they don't need to knock off 15 cows a year to keep me fed. Those cows are conceivably just as important on earth as any human being.

"The biggest change has been in my attitude toward myself and my fellow man. Perhaps this sounds crazy, but I'm not as agressive as I was in the past. There have been times in my life that I've wanted to go out and fight some guy for saying something to me. Or I'd scream and holler and really make an ass of myself. Now I catch myself smiling and trying to work out a problem. Vegetarianism has definitely had a mellowing effect on me."

It has been said that a vegetarian diet will increase longevity, particularly in that it helps prevent heart and vascular disease. Pearl isn't sure about this contention. "It's difficult to determine these things, but even if I do die at 50 or 55, my life has been vastly improved by vegetarian eating. Right now I'm putting in a more productive day than I ever have. I'm up every morning at 3:45 a.m. and I seldom go to bed before 10:00 p.m. Every hour of my day is filled completely, and I'm moving 100 miles per hour all the time."

While Pearl considers the positive effects of lacto-vegetarianism to be an overwhelming endorsement of that way of life, he does cite several negative aspects of vegetarianism. "It's very difficult to be invited out to people's homes to eat, because they tend to get uneasy about what to feed you. It's a little easier to entertain at your own home, but some individuals are wary of coming over to eat 18 pounds of rabbit food.

"If you're traveling a great deal—as I have been lately on behalf of the IFBB—you'll end up in restaurants eating mostly eggs and salads. I usually have a difficult time once I leave home, but it's not so inconvenient as to make me eat steak and hamburgers.

"Some experts note that vegetarians are not as strong as meat-eaters. While they may not be as strong in terms of the amount of weight they can push, vegetarians have a great deal more endurance than the average bodybuilder. And just because a person can push more weight doesn't mean he'll get more muscle."

Another common complaint is that vegetarians can't maintain muscle size, a contention that appears to be reinforced by Pearl's tremendous bodyweight losses after the '71 Universe. "Actually, my weight losses then—down to as low as 185—are totally misleading and weren't related to vegetarianism. Back in 1971, I was totally fed up with competing. Indeed, I hadn't even wanted to compete in the 1971 Universe, but everyone was badgering me about Arnold Schwarzenegger, so even at 41, I finally decided to give everyone a last shot at me. But after that was finished—due to my distaste for being pushed into competing—I never wanted to be in such a position again.

"When it was all over with, I didn't care about the trophy, the title or anything else, except being left alone. I figured that if I just totally ignored the sport—didn't even pose at exhibitions—and if I could change my image to look like a 'non-bodybuilder,' I'd get some peace and quiet. So, I began bicycle riding and fasted for weeks at a time to reduce my bodyweight. I wanted to weigh as little as possible so people would forget about me, which is exactly what happened.

"Once the possibility of doing exhibitions came up last year, I added weight quite easily on the vegetarian regimen. It was simply a matter of eating more calories—*not* necessarily more protein—and training heavier. Others have done the same thing. I understand that Mike Mentzer

was eating only about 45–50 grams of protein per day prior to the recent Southern Cup, at which he won looking bigger and more defined than ever."

Pearl does not suggest that anyone go on a lacto-vegetarian diet—or any type of vegetarian diet—unless he has a firm conviction to do so. "It's just like a religion or any other way of life. This kind of diet takes time to pay dividends, and to go on and off every few months is equivalent to a person stopping and starting smoking. He might as well have never stopped.

"I wouldn't presume to tell you to change to a vegetarian lifestyle, but if the concept interests you, I'd suggest you read as many books as possible on the subject before making up your mind. Why do you want to do this? Is it for

humanitarian reasons—do you not like to have animals killed to feed you? Is it for health? One of the best books I have read is *Are You Confused?* by Paavo Ariola. That book probably did as much to convert me to vegetarianism as anything I've ever read."

Bill Pearl also doesn't tell lacto-vegetarian bodybuilders what to eat. "I can only tell you how I eat, and you can take it from there. When I get up early in the morning to train—which suits my lifestyle—I might have a cup of mint tea as a perker-upper. Once back at home from the gym, I may have a cheese omelet, or five or six eggs prepared some other way. I might have a little cottage cheese, some heavy type of bran bread without butter, and another cup of tea.

"For lunch I'll have a large fresh salad, putting everything into it that I possibly can. The only dressing might be a small amount of oil and vinegar.

"At night my wife will cook some type of a souffle, or perhaps a casserole. I'll have another fresh salad and for dessert maybe some yogurt or fruit. My supplements include a good B-complex, E, C, kelp and zinc. I think that after the age of 40–45, zinc is very important for gland health. That's my total diet.

"Once you're eating as a vegetarian, you can't be swayed away from it by anyone, regardless of what he says. If a person offered me $50,000 to eat a steak, I'd tell him to stick it in his pocket. What's the sense of making a commitment if you're not committed? I'm a firm believer in sticking to convictions."

Protein and the Bodybuilder

by Armand Tanny

Not too long ago a surplus of protein was considered the mark of an affluent society. Nutrition experts were saying that people doing heavy physical work and eating a low protein diet would be in for a siege of malnutrition.

Now, however, many nutritionists are telling us that while protein is essential, its importance has been overstated; its prominence in the average diet far exceeds biological necessity.

Protein is the principle constituent of all plant and animal tissue (most of the solid matter in the human body is protein). Its importance is noted in the word itself—"protein" comes from the Greek *protos,* meaning "first."

This nutrient is essential for the building and replacement of body cells. Enzymes and hormones, which regulate many of the body's processes, are protein. So is hemoglobin. Protein also provides energy for the body, but it's utilized for that purpose only if the body has depleted its fat and carbohydrate energy stores.

According to studies, the more protein you eat every day, the more you need to eat in order to maintain your accumulated extra body weight. The U.S. Food and Nutrition Board's RDA (recommended daily allowance) for protein is 56 grams for a 154-pound man and 46 pounds for a 129-pound woman. Later research revealed that these figures were high, apparently because the people participating in the experiments were used to a high protein intake.

Many nutritional scientists now will tell you that if you're eating a calorically adequate diet, it's almost impossible not to have a sufficient protein intake. They feel that if all sources of experimental error were eliminated from protein requirement studies, the studies would show a daily protein requirement of 20–25 grams. And that wouldn't be 100% complete protein. Rather, it would be the type of protein (about 70% complete) which is consumed in the average American diet.

Excess protein in the system is not physiologically beneficial. Studies have apparently confirmed that a protein intake considerably lower than the U.S. Food and Nutrition Board's RDA can lead to improvements in high blood pressure and heart, artery and kidney disease.

Extensive research by the National Institute of Aging has revealed that too much protein speeds up the aging process. It does this by the extra demands it places on the metabolic processes.

A high-protein diet may also cause

osteoporosis by leaching the calcium from the bones—the calcium is then lost through the urine.

Of course, protein supplied in excess of the body's needs is converted to fat and stored. So the complication of obesity is added to the other problems.

Research, therefore, seems to have proved the dangers of a high-protein diet—but only for the nonathlete. Research information on the importance of the quantity and quality of protein in the diet of the hard-training athlete such as the bodybuilder is scanty and imprecise.

Dr. R. C. Darling and his co-workers at the Fatigue Laboratory, Harvard University, studied three groups of men engaged in physical work. The subjects ate a normal diet but the protein intake varied from group to group.

One group eating mainly potatoes, grains and vegetables had a protein intake of 50 grams per day. A second group eating mostly meat and high-protein foods consumed 157–192 grams per day. A third group took in 95–113 grams per day.

The Harvard studies showed that a male engaged in light activity needs 0.35 grams of protein per kilogram of body weight. Contrary to the claims of other studies, the Harvard group says that when the body is physically stressed through exercise, the demand for protein increases considerably. Men doing heavy physical work and eating a low-protein diet suffer decreases in their hemoglobin and other proteins in the blood.

The National Academy of Sciences has established a recommended daily allowance of 0.6 grams of protein per kilogram of body weight for adults if the protein consumed is of animal origin. For a standard mixed diet this agency recommends 0.8 grams of protein per kilogram of body weight per day. For a hardworking 200-pound man, that means 72 grams of protein a day.

Such statistics don't seem applicable to the hard-training bodybuilder who's pushing each set of an exercise to the point of pain. His work load is enormous, much greater than that of the average laborer. Recent experiments carried out by Drs. N. S. Scrimshaw and V. R. Young show that individuals on a three-month diet providing the National Academy of Sciences protein allowance mentioned above suffered decreases in muscle mass and, sometimes, changes in liver metabolism.

This leaves the bodybuilder up a tree. The National Academy of Science figures were established for adults engaged in non-bodybuilding activities that would burn approximately 3000 calories per day. The hard-training bodybuilder, however, will burn more than 5000 calories per day, so that his protein consumption will rise automatically unless he makes the mistake of getting those extra calories strictly through carbohydrate foods. Dr. Darling's investigations showed that his middle test group of men had the most satisfactory diet. This diet furnished each subject about 5000 calories and 95–113 grams of protein per day.

The athletes in Dr. Darling's Harvard studies were not bodybuilders training for a contest. The competition bodybuilder would likely command 50% more protein than the exercising people in the test group, bringing his protein consumption up to 150 grams per day.

In all likelihood the average American does not really need as much protein as he or she eats. One probable reason for the link between a high-protein diet and health in the minds of many people is the unconscious desire to justify our eating patterns. North Americans are hooked on high-protein foods.

The hard-training bodybuilder, on the other hand, requires much more protein than the amount suggested by the National Academy of Sciences and the U.S. Food and Nutrition Board. Even so, for the bodybuilder, a diet of unprocessed food consisting of meats, fruits, vegetables and dairy products—in quantities sufficient to satisfy his or her normal appetite—should provide all the protein necessary to build the body.

A Sensible Protein Diet for the Bodybuilder

by Armand Tanny

When you eat a steak, the meat is broken down in the mouth and stomach, then passed into the intestinal tract, where the blood absorbs the protein. The basic components of protein, called amino acids, are carried to the parts of the body where they are needed most—the brain, nervous system and the muscles.

The main advantage to eating steak is that animal tissue is a high-quality protein substance. This means that steak contains all eight of the essential animo acids that the body cannot produce on its own. While the body can produce the other 14 amino acids, it still must rely on outside sources for those vital eight.

The amount of protein an athlete needs on a daily basis is still debatable. However, recent studies have shown that a satisfactory diet for athletes consists of 5000 calories and 95–113 grams of protein a day. It's the concensus of competition bodybuilders, whose sport performance is measured by the quantity and quality of acquired muscle mass, that 150 grams of protein per day is a reasonable requirement.

In the early '70s meat was considered a miracle food, able to replenish an athlete's exhausted energy stores during hard training. When victorious athletes attributed their success to a diet made up only of meat, milk and eggs, food faddists claimed that large doses of protein were the best way to improve an athletic performance or to simply get in shape. Protein overload became synonymous with sports success. An athlete became a skilled performer simply because of diet.

It's not quite that simple, however. Protein is essential to any athlete's health and well-being, but protein per se won't ensure a winning edge in any sport. What matters more is the use your body makes of protein in your particular form of training. In running 20 miles or cycling 100 miles, the body will normally draw on reserves of liver glycogen which are supplied by carbohydrates and fat. When you get into your "second wind," you draw mostly on fat (less on carbohydrates) and begin to also utilize protein for energy production. Drawing on your protein reserves occurs as a last resort. However, there is evidence that bodybuilders in intense training utilize protein earlier in their workouts.

When a person starts to train or returns to training after a layoff, the body makes an increased demand for protein. The demand will level off at a certain point as long as the training intensity doesn't change. Among bodybuilders, an increased demand for protein is noticeable within a day after one adds an extra exercise to a regular routine, or even substitutes one exercise for another. An unaccustomed demand made upon a specific muscle changes the muscle's needs. Even a runner or cyclist would experience this increased protein demand if he switched to training on hills following a prolonged period of

training on a flat track. No studies have been made so far on protein consumption increases or decreases with respect to training routine changes, but alert athletes are aware of a fluctuation in appetite when such a change in routine occurs.

However, that doesn't mean necessarily that a drastic shift toward a protein-enriched diet is in order. The protein need will level off, perhaps at a slightly higher intake than before. One of the reasons for the increase is the loss of protein through the urine. Scientists think the loss is caused by stress to the red blood cells.

Because of this protein loss, the beginning bodybuilder should be careful not to do too much. Excess enthusiasm is perhaps the main cause of beginner dropouts. Instructors, also, may drive the novice too hard. The novice's body can't process excessive amounts of protein. The danger point is reached when the novice becomes too tired to eat, for the excessive stress to the red blood cells may cause anemia. Beginners in any endeavor should be carefully guided through initial stages of training. Workouts should be brief—a half-hour three times a week for several weeks is a good schedule. Even a few extra minutes of training in the workout are enough to cause fatigue that the body can't overcome with its limited ability to

Mike Mentzer is one of the most massive and densely developed bodybuilders. He believes in high-intensity workouts and in a protein-rich but well-balanced diet.

process the necessary protein. Psychologically speaking, the fatigue breaks down the will to continue training. Too much training can be devastating to the novice. It's better to undertrain than overtrain.

Eating regular, well-balanced meals and adding a high-protein drink each day is sufficient to carry the beginning bodybuilder through this stressful period. Within a few weeks, the shock of intense exercise will pass, and protein requirements will stabilize.

There is presently a widespread avoidance of red meat among athletes. If the protein found in red meat or dairy products doesn't contribute directly to athletic performance, it's frequently eliminated from the diet. Most serious bodybuilders, however, don't avoid red meat. This meat contains nitrogen and phosphorus, both of which are essential to good health.

The body is 20% protein by weight. Protein makes up the muscles, skin, hair, eyes, nails and teeth and is a major component of the blood, heart, lungs, brain and nerves. The blood hemoglobin that transports oxygen from the lungs to the body tissues, exchanging it for carbon dioxide, is comprised almost totally of protein. Protein is responsible for the production of enzymes and hormones that help digest food and regulate body processes. Protein also helps maintain the body's fluid balance. Though protein doesn't directly provide the energy required to do a workout, it remains the main constituent of muscle.

How does all this translate to the food an athlete eats? A half-pound steak contains 56 grams of protein. Since the hard-training bodybuilder needs about 150 grams of protein daily, that eight-ounce steak would hardly suffice. But the bodybuilder can supplement this with other animal and vegetable protein—e.g., eggs, fish, cheese, beans and seeds.

As you grow more conscious of your diet, and more aware of what foods contribute to your best performance, you become better able to measure your own protein intake. Some top athletes get the major share of their protein from red meat and protein drinks, while others get it from fish, eggs, protein supplements and dairy products. It's a matter of preference; whatever the athlete believes results in the best performance. Part of being an athlete is knowing your own body.

It's risky for an athlete, especially a bodybuilder, to avoid all animal protein, because usually a diet without meat, eggs, fish, cheese or milk doesn't contain all eight essential amino acids.

In order to supplement a meat or lacto-ovo-vegetarian diet (one which includes eggs and dairy products, besides vegetables) there are three basic complementary non-meat categories:

1. Grains and legumes
2. Grains plus milk products
3. Seeds plus legumes

These food combinations will ensure a balanced protein diet. At today's meat prices you might consider supplementing your regular diet with a combination of vegetable proteins and a protein supplement drink.

Red meat is an ideal protein, but it has a high level of saturated fats. Try to supplement your diet with fish and chicken, and consider using complementary vegetable proteins for some of your meals.

A survey of bodybuilders at the Mr. Olympia contest showed that during the final week or two of training, most of them avoided eating any red meat at all, primarily because of its fat content. However, for the average noncompetitive bodybuilder a diet of meat, fish, fowl, eggs, dairy products, vegetables, fruits, legumes, grains, seeds and a milk-egg-meat protein drink once or twice daily will provide the protein and all-around nutrition required.

If You Knew Tuna like I Know Tuna . . .

by Bill Dobbins

If you are what you eat, most bodybuilders must be made of tuna. Tuna (along with chicken and a few other kinds of fish) makes up the bulk of the diet of bodybuilders preparing for a contest. The reason is simple: tuna and the other foods mentioned are high in protein, low in fat and carbohydrate, and contain only moderate amounts of calories. But buying the right kind of tuna and preparing it in a variety of ways so you don't go crazy from boredom isn't that easy.

Canned tuna comes in a number of varieties. Some people prefer all white tuna, other don't mind the dark, but the main distinction to be aware of is the difference between tuna packed in water and in oil.

Oil, as I've said in previous articles, contains a lot of calories. A tablespoon of vegetable oil (or butter or margarine) provides about 100 calories. Therefore, when you open a can of tuna that has been packed in oil, you are dealing with the calories contained in both the fish and the oil.

On a recent visit to a supermarket, I picked up a can of tuna packed in oil. It listed the calories contained as 490, the protein as 80 grams and fat as 30 grams. A can of tuna packed in water, on the other hand, contained only 240 calories, 43 grams of protein and four grams of fat. Both cans were 12½ ounces, and both sold for the same price.

Let's look at the two cans side by side:

	Calories	Protein	Fat
Oil	490	80	30
Water	240	43	4

Although the tuna packed in oil contained almost twice the protein, it also had more than twice the calories and 7½ times the fat. Protein is good for building muscles, but most bodybuilders preparing for a contest are interested in getting cut up, not putting on a lot of bulk, so eating tuna packed in oil is obviously not a good idea.

It's said, "You get what you pay for." That also applies with tuna. Next to the 12½-ounce can of tuna in water there was another brand, with a 13-ounce can, that sold for a little more. In fact, the 13-ounce can was cheaper ounce for ounce. But what do you get for your money?

Calories	Protein	Fat
460	97	8

This brand is obviously higher in calories than the other (although still lower in calories than the tuna packed in oil) and it contains a great deal of protein while being only a little higher in

fat content. The point is: tuna varies tremendously from brand to brand, so read the labels and decide what is best for your training regimen.

But once you've bought your tuna, you have to consider how to prepare it. Tuna, meal after meal, can really get to be a drag. But you don't want to mix it with anything that will spoil it as a contest food, so that limits your range of choices.

Valerie Coe, Boyer Coe's wife, is heavily into weight training. Boyer eats a lot of tuna, and Valerie has given considerable thought to how those meals can be kept palatable and interesting.

Here are a few of her favorite tuna recipes:

Breakfast

7½ ounces of tuna
1 tablespoon low-fat yogurt (or safflower
  mayonnaise)
½ diced, medium apple
⅛ cup raisins
⅛ cup walnuts, chopped fine

Lunch

7½ ounces of tuna
Diced onion (whatever amount desired)
1 tablespoon pickle relish
2 cherry tomatoes, cut in four pieces

or (for a less-restricted diet):

7½ ounces of tuna
1 tablespoon diced black olives
Onion and pickle relish (as above)
Chopped celery
Shredded carrots

There are a million other ways to spice up your tuna meals; it just takes a little imagination to discover them. To give you a head start, two of your basic helpers can be potatoes and rice.

Potatoes are one of the most maligned of foods. Dieters think they are high in calories because so many people cover them with things like butter and sour cream. In fact, a medium-sized baked potato contains only 80–90 calories. If you ate nothing but potatoes, you probably couldn't eat enough to keep your weight up, much less gain any.

Mixed with tuna, potatoes provide a nutritious,

Boyer Coe, winner of the 1981 World Cup.

low-calorie treat. Here's one way to combine them:

Bake one medium potato (425 degrees for about 1 hour)
Meantime, saute in Pam or other vegetable spray:
  Chopped onion (or shallots)
  Chopped mushrooms
When potato is cooked, cut off enough of the top to allow you to scoop out the potato from the skin. Leave enough inside so that skin won't tear.

Combine potato with onion, mushroom and tuna, fill potato skin, sprinkle with parmesan cheese, and bake in oven for 25 minutes at 350 degrees.

Rice is a less nutritious food than potatoes, but it does lend itself to combination with tuna. Here the variety is endless—mixing tuna and rice with mushrooms, peas, onions; flavoring with soy sauce, etc. As long as you keep your portions under control, there is no reason why you cannot keep up muscular bulk and get cut up on a diet that includes these foods.

Another possibility, of course, is salads. Make up a plate of lettuce, tomatoes, cucumbers, mushrooms, various other kinds of vegetables, and top it off with a scoop of tuna for taste, protein and fiber.

Tuna, as I said above, is only one low-fat protein source. There are many other kinds of

fish, as well as chicken and other varieties of poultry, that you can add to your diet. The idea is simply this: just because you are trying to diet, there is no reason to torture yourself. You can keep your weight down and still enjoy your meals.

Boyer Coe makes it a point these days to stay as close as possible to contest weight all the time, which means a heck of a lot of dieting. That is why he is so concerned with keeping his meals interesting; otherwise, the discipline could just get too hard to handle. You can do the same.

Getting into the Egg Habit

by Joe Weider

The egg is one of the most versatile and nutritious of foods, as well as probably the best source of complete protein.

We have recipes for egg dishes dating as far back as the ancient Egyptians. Louis XIII was renowned for being able to cook eggs 100 different ways.

The great thing about eggs is that you can let loose and really be creative without worrying about creating a disaster. This is of great benefit to a bodybuilder on an otherwise fairly monotonous diet.

Bodybuilders like eggs for a number of reasons. An egg gives you about six grams of protein and only 80 calories. While each egg contains six grams of fat, it also provides a great deal of lecithin, which is instrumental in breaking down cholesterol in the body.

Eggs have an abundance of calcium (approximately 27 mg/egg) and are also high in Vitamin A (590 I.U./egg). But it's easy for the nutritional value of eggs to be adversely affected, although most people aren't aware of this fact. The way you cook or don't cook eggs can make all the difference.

For instance, a lot of athletes are fond of eating their eggs raw. Wrong. This is a bad idea for a number of reasons. For one thing, it takes time for the stomach to digest protein. Therefore, a protein food has to remain in the stomach long enough for it to do its work. Raw eggs, or even those that are merely undercooked, pass through the digestive system so quickly that the body is able to get little of the nutritional value.

But there are other reasons why eating eggs raw is a bad idea. For example, raw egg white contains a substance called avadin, which combines with biotin (one of the B vitamins), preventing it from reaching the blood. Persons deficient in biotin become ill, mentally depressed and suffer from eczema.

Another problem concerns undigested protein, which may cause allergies when it reaches the blood. Unfortunately, albumen, the protein of egg white, dissolves in water or digestive juices and may pass into the blood undigested. A lot of well-meaning mothers have produced allergies and eczema in their children by regularly feeding them soft-cooked eggs.

Eggs need to be cooked until the white is no

longer a semiliquid and the yolk is at least slightly firm. But they also need to be cooked away from the light, because when eggs are fried or scrambled uncovered, as much as 48% of the Vitamin B$_2$ can be destroyed. And just think how often you have eaten eggs that have been cooked in a frying pan without a cover!

The basic way to prepare an egg, of course, is to boil it. But have you ever heard the expression, "She couldn't boil an egg." Well, boiling an egg is not that easy.

If you boil it too long at too high a temperature, the inside becomes tough and you're left with an unpleasant ring resulting from a breakdown of the sulphur compounds in the yolk. If you don't boil it long enough, the egg white will tend to pull apart when you try to remove the shell.

Getting just the right cooking time and the right texture to your egg depends on a number of things: how cold the egg was when you started; how hot the water was; how much water you used; and how many eggs you cooked at the same time. All this can be very complicated, but there are a few shortcuts.

Eggs cook better when they are at room temperature, rather than just out of the refrigerator, when you put them in the water. To make sure they don't get tough, try boiling some

water, turning off the heat, slipping in the eggs, bringing the water back to a boil, then turning off the heat and letting the eggs sit. They will soft boil in approximately 10 minutes and hard boil in a little over 20 minutes.

Another method is to put the eggs in cold water and slowly bring the water to a boil. Then turn off the heat and let the eggs sit. They will soft boil in about five minutes. It will take almost 20 minutes for them to hard boil by this method.

If you're more traditionally minded, and prefer to keep the heat on under the pot, don't leave the heat on for the entire cooking period. Leave it on perhaps four minutes for a six-minute egg or six minutes for a hard-boiled egg. Then let the eggs sit for the rest of the required time (which you will have to figure out for yourself). By turning the heat off for the latter part of the cooking process, you will get a better egg.

Incidentally, the way to keep eggs from breaking in the pot while you are boiling them is to: (1) make sure they are at room temperature when you put them in the water; (2) take the pot off the flame when you are adding the eggs; (3) best of all, use a wire basket or strainer inside the pot to keep the eggs from touching the bottom.

A lot of people like fried eggs, but they avoid them because of the calories and the saturated

fat in the cooking oil or butter. The answer lies in the new vegetable oil sprays on the market. These products (Pam is the best known, but there are others) usually contain lecithin oil or vegetable oil, and they add very few calories or fat to the food you are cooking. Another possibility is the Teflon-type frying pan, which doesn't require the use of a liquid as a frying agent. These pans require a lot of care to keep them in perfect shape, but they do work.

When frying eggs, remember to keep them covered as much as possible. Also, the lower the heat and the longer you let the egg cook at very low temperature, the less you are going to toughen the protein. The ideal combination, therefore, is to fry the egg slowly in a covered utensil.

Poaching eggs is also a popular method of preparation. To poach eggs satisfactorily, you must use fresh eggs. The whites of older eggs will run when dropped into the water.

To poach an egg, get the water boiling, turn off the heat, and break the egg into the water. Cover the utensil and then use just enough heat to keep the water simmering. The egg will cook in about eight minutes. If you turn the heat off entirely, let the egg sit in the water for a full 15 minutes.

Eggs cooked like this taste great when served on a piece of whole wheat toast. Incidentally, you don't need to drown the eggs when you're poaching them. An inch of water in the pan is enough.

Scrambled eggs, another favorite, can be a problem to a bodybuilder in a number of ways. For one thing, when you have to constantly manipulate the eggs in the pan, you run into the problem of exposure to light. For another, a lot of recipes (including some used by restaurants) add a lot of things like cream and butter to enhance the taste. This means extra fat and calories. If you do scramble eggs, keep them on a low flame, use vegetable spray instead of butter, and try adding powdered milk to enrich them rather than cream or butter.

By the way, anyone who prefers frying or scrambling in the normal way should always use butter instead of oil. Oil cooks eggs at such a high temperature that it can turn them into shoe leather.

The natural alternative to scrambling eggs is the omelette. There is no limit to the number of variations that you can create when making this dish. Almost anything goes.

The traditional French omelette is fairly easy to make. Break three eggs into a mixing bowl and beat them together with one tablespoon of cold water and a little salt and pepper.

Omelettes are best made in an omelette pan, which has sloping sides that allow you to turn and fold the omelette when you are finished cooking it. Another way to cook omelettes is on a large grill. Obviously, an electric frying pan with a cover would also be a good method.

Although the "low-slow" cooking method applies to omelettes as well as any other egg dish, there is a tradition for "high-fast" omelette preparation. Some chefs claim that an omelette cooked in only 20–30 seconds doesn't have time to get tough. I am not really sure if this is true or not.

In any event, when making an omelette, add your vegetable spray to the pan and then pour in the beaten eggs. Swish them around until they cover the whole pan. The bottom will become firm fairly quickly, leaving some uncooked liquid on top. Lift the edge of the cooked part and let the liquid flow under by tilting the pan. After you do this one or two times, there will be just a slight amount of liquid egg on top. You can leave this. It will cook when you fold the omelette.

What makes an omelette interesting is what you put in it. This, as I said, can be almost anything—I'll discuss this shortly. Whatever you want to use in the omelette, place it in the center of the pan and fold the edges of the omelette over it, much the way you would fold a letter into three sections. If the omelette resists folding, hold it together with the spatula for a few moments and it should stay in place.

Now comes the part where most people have their difficulties. Hold the serving plate in one hand, place the edge of the omelette pan against the top of the plate, and then quickly invert the pan so that the omelette rests bottom side up on the plate. Purists can tuck the bottom of the omelette in on each side to make it look plumper. It helps to use a paper towel to do this since the omelette will be hot.

Turning to the question of what to put in your omelette, bodybuilders have less choice than most people since they will want to avoid high-fat fillings like cheese and sour cream. But that still leaves a whole lot. Try, for example, sauteing (in another pan) some onions, green peppers, mushrooms and a little garlic. This makes a great addition to an omelette. Cooked spinach, seafood and even Chinese vegetables can also be used to create unusual and tasty omelettes. Let's

face it, a bodybuilder can use all of the high-protein, low-fat, moderate-calorie dishes he can find, and there is virtually nothing that fills the bill as well as an omelette.

What we've been talking about here, of course, does not exhaust the methods that can be used in preparing eggs. They can be steamed and baked, as well as added to any number of other dishes to increase the protein and nutritional content. You can use eggs in almost any way you want, providing you follow the few simple rules to keep them tender and protect their nutritional value.

But I'd like to leave you with my absolute favorite egg recipe, courtesy of Michel Geurard's book, *Cuisine Minceur*. You want to impress somebody for breakfast sometime? Try scrambled eggs—with caviar!

To serve four:
  4 fresh eggs
  2 teaspoons of fromage blanc (see below)
  1 teaspoon of finely minced onion
  1 teaspoon of minced chives
  Salt and pepper
  1 ounce, or 4 generous teaspoons, of caviar

Fromage Blanc:
  Low-fat diet ricotta cheese
  Low-fat yogurt
  Salt

Put 1½ cups ricotta and four level tablespoons of yogurt in the electric blender. Add pinch of salt. Blend mixture until cheese is pureed, with no trace of graininess. Store covered in refrigerator for 12 hours before using.

Directions:
Using a serrated knife, carefully saw off the round ends of the four eggs. Empty only three of the eggs into a bowl and put the contents of the fourth aside for another use. Wash the shells and their caps carefully in hot water and set them cut sides down on a cloth to dry.

(Note: This is not really very difficult to do, but all four shells may not be cut perfectly at the first try. We suggest that it is more convenient, if you use eggs for something else a day or two before, to cut some or all four shells in advance. Wash them, store them in a little cold water in the refrigerator, then rinse them again and let them dry before using.)

Beat together the three eggs and strain them to remove any scraps of shell and the filaments in the whites. In a heavy-bottomed saucepan, scramble the eggs over moderate heat until they become a thick, almost smooth cream.

Remove the pan from the heat and, still beating with a whisk, add the fromage blanc, onion and chives, and season to taste with salt and pepper.

Spoon the scrambled eggs into the egg shells, add a spoonful of caviar to each shell, and set the caps on top. The caviar should be just visible under the cap. Set the eggs in egg cups and serve immediately.

Sounds complicated? It sure is. But what a taste! The thing is that not too many people care to go to so much trouble. For those who do, enjoy this taste treat. For the rest, let me leave you with something a little more practical—my idea for a quick, high-protein omelette in the morning:

Beat together two or three eggs. Add pepper, chopped onions (fresh or dried), chopped mushrooms (fresh, canned or dried), and paprika.

Use this mixture to make an omelette. In the center, place a small amount of cottage cheese.

Optional: Small amount of soy sauce (if you can stand brown-looking eggs).

Milk and Milk Products

Something for Every Body?

by Joe Weider

Milk. It's the first food we taste when we come into the world, and one of the best, most complete foods anyone can imagine. It contains protein, calcium and lots of Vitamin A. Milk is used in sauces, desserts. In powdered form, it supplies the protein needs of underdeveloped countries. We can it, condense it, evaporate it, and make cheese and yogurt out of it.

Unfortunately, to a large percentage of the world's population, milk is all but a poison. Milk is difficult for humans to digest. In order to handle it, our bodies use a special enzyme that breaks down the lactose in milk products. Virtually all (but not absolutely all) babies have an abundance of this enzyme. But many adults do not, and they develop *lactose intolerance*, which is simply an inability to digest whole milk. Some races are more widely affected by this condition than others. Caucasians suffer from lactose intolerance the least. Blacks are subject to it more frequently, and Asians and Orientals still more. When this condition exists, milk is definitely *not* for everybody—despite what Pat Boone may tell us.

And there is a widespread body of opinion that whole milk is not a suitable food for *any* adult, except in special circumstances. It is simply too rich. A cup of whole milk contains 160 calories, nine grams of fat and 12 of carbohydrate. The fat and cholesterol in milk have been linked with heart disease and are suspect in certain cancers. Bodybuilders don't need to know this to shy away from milk; they know it tends to make you fat, and that's enough.

Since modern society is so weight conscious, milk producers have come up with alternate products. One of these is so-called "low-fat" milk. Certainly, this represents a step in the right direction. But there are various degrees of "low-fatness" in milk. Most of the time the reduction in fat and calories is only 50% or so. Much better, it would seem, is nonfat milk, which is traditionally known as skim milk.

Nonfat milk is just that—milk containing virtually no fat at all. Instead of 160 calories, a cup of nonfat milk only contains about 90 calories, and its calcium content is greater than that of whole milk. There is a loss, however. You get only 10 I.U. of Vitamin A as opposed to 350 I.U. But that's a small price to pay.

Nonfat milk makes a good addition to the diet of any bodybuilder. The protein and calcium content, coupled with the lack of fat, makes it an ideal food. There is still the matter of lactose intolerance, however.

To anyone who cannot digest even nonfat milk, there are other possibilities open. Milk products can be eaten and digested by people who cannot handle whole milk. One popular milk product is cheese. Unfortunately, cheese can also be high in calories and fat content. The best-known way around this is cottage cheese. The dry-cured variety has only 62 calories and .31 grams of fat per half cup.

Another acceptable form of cheese is mozzarella. If you look for the kind that's made from skim milk, you will find you are getting only 79 calories and 4.51 grams of fat per ounce, which is about half of what you get when you eat cheddar cheese.

Yogurt is another popular milk substitute. The calorie and fat content depends on what kind of yogurt you buy and how you serve it. Yogurt made from whole milk and sweetened with fruit and sugar by the manufacturer is a serious no-no for the bodybuilder, or anyone interested in moderating the diet. Plain low-fat yogurt contains about 144 calories and 3.52 grams of fat per eight ounces. If you like it sweet, add your own ingredients. Add some strawberries, for instance, or slices of orange. If you are really cutting down on calories, try yogurt flavored with low-cal jelly.

Just because whole milk is so fattening, don't overlook the protein, calcium and other nutritional benefits of milk products. But try to stick to products made from skim milk, and avoid the so-called "imitation dairy products."

If you go to a restaurant and they don't have milk or half-and-half, don't use the phony milk imitation—at least, not if you are trying to get into serious contest shape. Most of these products contain some kind of vegetable fat. They are also full of chemicals and flavor ingredients.

By and large, you don't know what you are getting when you put milk substitutes into your coffee. When you are shopping at a supermarket, take the trouble to check the labels of various milk substitutes and find out what is in them. You will probably decide that, if you need something in your coffee, it's better to go with a tablespoon of half-and-half than to fill yourself up with vegetable fat and chemicals.

There's one other way of getting the nutritional benefits of milk, and that's by using the powdered variety. Powdered milk can be added to a variety of recipes, thereby raising the nutritional content. One cup of dry, nonfat instant milk contains 245 calories, virtually no fat, and *879 mg of calcium*. And this amount of powdered milk is just about enough to make one full quart when reconstituted.

Powdered milk can be added to drinks, stews, casseroles and lots of other dishes. It makes sauces richer and more tasty, with no addition of fat. It does add calories, however, so take that into consideration.

To give you one example of how powdered milk can be used to enrich your cooking, I would like to pass on a recipe for meat loaf from Adelle Davis' *Let's Cook It Right*.

Saute lightly:
    1 chopped onion
    1 chopped green pepper or pimiento
    1 minced clove garlic
Remove from heat and add:
    1 pound ground beef (lean variety, or grind it
        yourself)
    1 egg
    ½ cup wheat germ
    3 tablespoons ground parsley
    ⅓ cup powdered milk
    ¼ to ½ teaspoon freshly ground black
        peppercorns
    3 teaspoons salt
    ½ cup nonfat milk
    Pinch each of thyme and basil

Mix thoroughly, preferably with fingertips; mold into a loaf in a shallow baking dish or pack into an oiled loaf pan; sprinkle generously with paprika; bake in moderate oven at 350 degrees F about 40 minutes, or until temperature in center is 185 degrees F; insert thermometer when loaf is nearly done.

Electrolytes

by Joe Weider

If you are into training, you are going to sweat. That is nature's neat way of keeping you cool in a hot situation. If you jog, swim, cycle, climb a mountain or romp in the hay, you are going to lose water. You lose water when you breathe, and you lose it through normal excretion as well.

However, such activities remove more than water from your body. They also remove considerable amounts of potassium, sodium, magnesium and calcium—electrolytes vital to a properly functioning body. These elements are called salts. These salts in your body affect how much you weigh, the beat of your heart, your blood pressure and the ability of your muscles to contract during a long workout.

The vital characteristic of the body salts sodium and potassium is their ability to separate into ions when they are in solution. Table salt, for example, which is sodium chloride, separates into ions when it is in solution. The sodium ion has a positive charge (+) and the chloride ion has a negative (–) charge. These salt solutions have the ability to conduct electricity, and for this reason they are called electrolytes. The process of creating electricity is the same in your car battery through the ionization of elements like lead and sulphur. In effect, we are walking batteries.

The electrical behavior of the two main elements, sodium and potassium, in the body cells is basic to life. The transmission of nerve impulses and the function of muscle depends entirely on the conducting ability of these elements within the largely liquid makeup of the body.

A nerve impulse is moved along by the migration of sodium and potassium ions. The membrane surrounding a cell acts as a filter. This membrane separates the normally present potassium within the cell from the sodium outside the cell. Water moves freely through the cell membrane, but the electrolytes dare not cross this border unless given the signal. When an impulse occurs in a nerve fiber, the cell membrane suddenly becomes permeable. The potassium ions are able to pass through the membrane filter and get outside the cell while the sodium ions manage to get inside the cell. This movement takes place in an instant (because it's an electrical transmission) and causes the electrical characteristics of the nerve fiber to change as the impulse is passed along. The heart muscle fibers depend on this process through the specialized conducting tissue inside the heart that controls the heart rate.

In the process of returning cells to their normal state, with the sodium departing the cell and the potassium coming back, the movement creates electrical energy. It is this electrical cycle that stimulates the heart to beat and makes muscles contract. No wonder that the potassium

content of the heart muscle fibers is so important. In fact, when potassium is low, the heart tends to add extra beats or beat irregularly. During open heart surgery, the heart can be stopped by injecting an excess amount of potassium into the blood stream. The overload of potassium in solution outside the heart prevents the potassium inside the heart muscle fibers from passing through the membrane filter to the outside and completely inhibits the electrical activity of the heart cells. This electrical quiet results in total cardiac arrest. The motionless heart is a better surgical bet.

Athletes and other physically active people often experience the muscle cramps that result from an excessive sodium loss. Muscle cramps are a common manifestation of salt loss, and fatigue is a common symptom of salt depletion in healthy people. Fatigue occurs where salt loss is related to a disease, such as Addison's disease, which is caused by adrenal insufficiency. Victims crave salt and are low on energy. The adrenal insufficiency must be corrected to treat the disease.

Pre-contest cramps are a common occurrence among bodybuilders. It has been the custom a few days before a contest for contestants to cut down on water intake in the hope of sharpening their definition. This loss, compounded by continual heavy training, results in cramps.

Most of the sodium is outside the body cells. The amount of sodium in the blood and tissues outside the cells has the concentration of seawater, a condition that underscores the theory that we had our origins in the sea. Inside the cell itself the main salt is potassium.

The potassium inside the cells is directly involved in cell metabolism, the breakdown of carbohydrates and the products from carbohydrates, fats and proteins. Potassium within the cell is represented as a salt of potassium and hydrogen phosphate. The phosphate is essential in the formation of ATP, phosphate radicals that contain the energy your cells need. ATP supplies the energy needed during the first 10 seconds of any muscular movement before the muscle switches over to the utilization of glycogen.

The amount of water the body retains is directly related to the retention of sodium. If your body retains 1200 mg of sodium chloride, of which 468 mg is pure sodium, it will retain one liter of water (2.2 pounds). When the body loses sodium it loses water, and when it retains sodium it retains water. In this way the

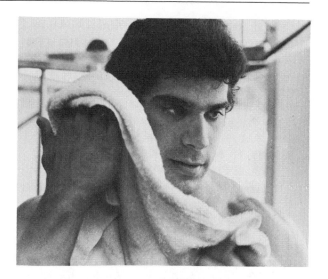

Pooped halfway through a workout? Then learn the energy secret of champions like Lou Ferrigno and Arnold Schwarzenegger!

concentration of sodium in solution outside the cell is maintained near the normal concentration of seawater. Sodium is absorbed by the small intestine and the stomach, and is carried by the blood to the kidneys, where it is filtered out and returned to the blood in amounts needed to maintain blood levels of sodium required by the body. The absorption of sodium requires energy. Ninety-five percent of the sodium we normally ingest is excessive and is excreted in the urine. The adrenal glands regulate sodium metabolism. Too much salt in food interferes with the absorption and utilization of protein.

Sodium deficiencies are uncommon because nearly all foods contain it. The conversion of

carbohydrates into fat for digestion is impaired when sodium is absent. Sodium keeps the other blood minerals soluble so that they will not build up as deposits in the bloodstream. It acts with the chlorine to improve blood and lymph health, helps purge carbon dioxide from the body and aids in hydrochloric acid production in the stomach.

Sodium is found in all foods. Kelp is an excellent supplemental source of sodium.

Many reducing gimmicks rely on the dehydration associated with the loss of sodium in the body. Such diuretics will cause sodium excretion with the resultant loss of body fluid, and hence, an apparent loss of body weight. The weight loss, however, is water, not fat, and as soon as the body regains its normal sodium content, the body weight is back up to the original. Certain diseases that cause sodium retention subsequently cause body water retention, and swelling develops. Estrogen, the female hormone, causes salt retention and the tissue swelling associated with menstrual cycles.

Sodium and water retention may also indicate serious heart trouble. Fluid accumulates and makes breathing difficult. Other kidney and liver diseases will cause sodium-associated fluid retention and swelling.

Normally the kidneys eliminate excess sodium. However, excessive salt intake on a daily basis can overwhelm the kidneys' ability to do this, resulting in chronic sodium toxicity manifested by the usual tissue swelling.

It is easy enough to get rid of the excess sodium by using a diuretic. The problem is that potassium is flushed out along with it, resulting in a potassium deficiency.

The bodybuilder should be particularly careful about prolonging a low carbohydrate diet. The absence of carbohydrate causes the kidneys to eliminate sodium, which causes body fluid loss and an apparent loss of weight. But the weight loss is water and not fat. As soon as a normal amount of carbohydrate is eaten again, the normal sodium and its associated water level are reestablished, and the weight loss from water elimination is reversed.

Even bed rest, through complex mechanisms, causes the elimination of sodium and water with a subsequent loss of body weight. That is why people feel faint when they first get up from a long stay in bed.

Although it might be difficult to believe the amount, the average American ingests three to seven grams of sodium and six to 18 grams of sodium chloride (NaCl) each day, far in excess of the basic requirement of .2 mg. Anything in excess of 14 grams of salt daily is an invitation to trouble.

Potassium is also linked to carbohydrate metabolism. It connects the basic amino acids together to form polypeptides that constitute the protein for body growth and development. As mentioned earlier, it stimulates nerve impulses for muscular contraction (ATP). It preserves the proper alkalinity of the body fluids, and stimulates the kidneys to eliminate waste. Along with sodium, it normalizes the heartbeat and nourishes the muscular system. It unites with phosphorus to supply oxygen to the brain, and functions with calcium to regulate neuromuscular activity.

When the salt intake is high and the potassium intake is low, there is a greater tendency to develop high blood pressure. Because sodium and potassium must be in balance, the excessive use of salt depletes the body's scarce potassium supply. In any event, the disparity caused by the excess salt, according to recent studies, is evidently responsible for the large percentage of people with high blood pressure, and, therefore, it's a contributing factor in heart attacks and strokes.

The amount of sodium your body requires can be obtained through normal eating of unprocessed food daily. The kidneys efficiently eliminate or retain sodium according to the body's needs. On the other hand, potassium loss cannot be controlled by the kidneys. Studies show that we consume far too much sodium and not enough potassium. First of all, we add too much salt to our food. But worse, valuable sources of potassium are lost through food processing where salt is used to increase the taste. Thus you continue to get overdosed with salt and undersupplied with potassium. Inadvertently, you ingest a lot of hidden sodium in a processed food diet. One only has to browse through a supermarket and read the labels on all foods that are wrapped, packaged or canned to realize the prevalence of salt and the seeming impossibility of controlling its intake. The problem can be quickly remedied by using only fresh fruits, vegetables and meats.

Potassium constitutes 5% of the total mineral content of the body. Large amounts of potassium are found in potato skins, bananas and green leafy vegetables. Whole grains, sunflower seeds and mint leaves are also good sources.

Potassium is rapidly absorbed from the small

intestine and is excreted through urination and perspiration. Little is lost through the feces. It can also be depleted by using diuretics, a fact the bodybuilder should consider when attempting to cut up for contests.

Coffee and alcohol increase the urinary excretion of potassium. Alcohol compounds the damage because it also depletes the magnesium reserve. Magnesium plays a large part in carbohydrate, fat and protein production. Aldosterone, an adrenal hormone, stimulates potassium excretion, which subsequently makes the excess intake of sugar antagonistic toward potassium. Since excessive sugar intake can, paradoxically, cause low blood sugar, it creates a stressful condition that strains the adrenal glands, causing additional potassium to be lost in the urine while water and salt are held in the tissues. Refined sugar can cause the urine to become alkaline so that minerals cannot be held in solution. A further deficiency can be caused by vomiting, diarrhea and both physical and mental stress.

A potassium deficiency impairs glucose metabolism and, without the needed converted glycogen, the muscles tend to become paralyzed. Further, a deficiency may cause nervous disorders, insomnia and constipation. People suffering from diseases of the digestive tract are frequently found to be potassium-deficient. Potassium loss occurs also when taking hormone products such as cortisone or aldosterone. Potassium deficiency can cause poor reflexes and soft, sagging muscles, the condition totally counter to bodybuilding.

Potassium is indicated in treatment of high blood pressure, diabetes and headache-causing allergies. Therapeutic doses are sometimes used to slow the heartbeat in severe cases of injury, such as burns.

The hard-training bodybuilder should make an effort to modify his diet so it includes more potassium and less ordinary salt. Meats contain a considerable amount of potassium and are reasonably low in sodium. Meat is largely cellular, hence its potassium content. Fish, beef, pork or chicken contain about five times more sodium than potassium. Foods like processed meats are heavyweights in the sodium department. Weiners, for example, contain about five times as much sodium as potassium. In preparing meat for cooking, it is best to use salt-free condiments. If there is a need for additional flavor, then try roasting meat or fish with fruit.

Whether you are getting sufficient potassium

in the fruits and vegetables that you eat depends on whether they are raw, cooked, canned or frozen. Most of the salted, canned stuff contains much more sodium than potassium. You can avoid that by cooking your own fresh vegetables. Use salt-free spices for seasoning. Beans are particularly high in potassium and should be cooked without salt. All fresh fruits contain potassium. Bananas are an especially good source.

You have to be careful about butter, margarine and the processed cheeses because of the heavy salt content. Unprocessed grain products will remain high in potassium. Prepared cereals have an altered ratio of sodium to potassium, resulting in the usual extreme imbalance.

As mentioned earlier, you should attempt to improve your potassium intake and control your salt intake to a reasonable extent. For most people that means preparing your own food

seasoned with something other than table salt, and eating plenty of fresh fruits and vegetables. If you must have salt for your taste, there is a condiment (put out by the Morton Salt Company) called Lite Salt, which is a 50-50 mixture of potassium and sodium. The alternative is to use diuretics, which in turn deplete the potassium as well as the sodium and create a condition that must be treated. Proper eating is the ultimate way to maintain a healthy balance between sodium and potassium.

During competition training, a bodybuilder needs to replace fluids and vital elements lost in excretion and sweating. They should be replaced quickly. Such an electrolyte drink has been developed especially for the bodybuilder by the Weider Research Clinic. Called the *Dynamic Stamina Builder*, it replaces the fluids and elements, along with providing glucose for renewed energy and quick absorption without discomfort. The ingredients in this electrolyte refresher are important, but it is the proper

balance between them that makes them comfortable to assimilate. This crystal powder, when mixed with water, helps prevent cramps and reduces muscle fatigue. It contains no artificial sweeteners or preservatives.

Long-distance runners are known to "hit the wall" after about two hours of running. This is apparently due to the depletion of energy stores and the muscle failure caused by the electrolyte imbalance from water loss. The bodybuilder, especially in countdown training for a contest, is likely to experience this same phenomenon after a couple hours of work. It becomes a mental and emotional ordeal to release more energy in order to continue training.

It is worth anyone's while to drink a half glass of Dynamic Stamina Builder every 20 minutes or so during the workout. Flavorful, it goes down and stays down and helps maintain that vital sodium-potassium balance that prevents fatigue and keeps those muscles contracting fully with extended energy.

Seasonings

by Bill Dobbins

Nutrition writers like to compare food to fuel, as if people were some sort of automobile and food no more than biological gasoline. But food means a lot more to people than a mere energy source. We often overeat, and eat the wrong things, which proves that we're driven by motives much more complex than a simple desire to satisfy our energy needs.

Good cooks have always understood this. They know food should appeal to all of our senses if we're to get maximum enjoyment out of it. This means it should look good, smell good, and be attractively displayed when served.

But the fundamental quality we expect from our food is good taste. Our taste buds have the ability to recognize a wide variety of tastes and flavors, and a good cook plays upon this ability the way a musician uses the whole range of his instrument to entertain us.

Unfortunately, many of the subtlest and most enjoyable flavors do not exist in most of the foods we eat. Therefore, to make our meals more palatable—especially when on the limited sort of diet that most bodybuilders have to follow to get in contest shape—those flavors have to be added to our foods to make them really tasty. This is done by the use of seasonings.

Many people don't really understand how seasonings work. When you add spices or herbs to food, the aromatic oils in the seasoning account for the added flavor. These are not actually oils, but alcohols and similar substances which evaporate very easily. Therefore, the trick is to keep them in the seasonings until used, and then to see that they don't escape from the food when the seasoning has been applied.

The way seasonings work on hot foods is comparable to the way coffee beans or tea leaves behave in water to produce a beverage. Preparing these beverages, you steep the coffee beans or tea leaves in hot water until the aromatic oils inside them pass into the water. This is exactly what happens when you add parsley, sage, rosemary, thyme or any other seasoning to a hot dish like stew, soup or a sauce.

The aromatic oils in seasonings pass into hot foods in just a few minutes, which means that you should add the seasoning toward the end of cooking. If you leave the seasoning in hot food too long the oils evaporate, which makes for a great smell in the kitchen but little taste in the food.

With cold foods it's another matter. It takes at least a half hour for the oils in most seasonings to pass into cold dishes. That's why a lot of

recipes require that you let the food sit in the refrigerator for several hours or even overnight. For instance, putting chives in cottage cheese makes that essentially bland food a lot tastier, but you have to allow it to sit long enough for the seasoning to do its work.

Adding seasonings and flavorings to food does not increase the caloric content of the dish, and can allow you to cut back on sugar and other high-calorie additions without adversely affecting the taste of the food.

There are some disadvantages to certain kinds of seasonings, however. Salt, for example, used to excess, can contribute to hypertension and tends to make the body retain excess water. However, a small amount of salt is necessary to human life.

A dish that was properly seasoned when it was being prepared will taste just fine without any further additions. When you are being served a meal by a good cook, there should be no reason to have salt and pepper on the dinner table. In fact, adding these spices without tasting the dish first is considered a premier insult by a good cook.

For those who like "hot," spicy food, but who are afraid that sharp spices are bad for the digestive system, it should be pointed out that the digestive tract of a healthy person is covered with a thick coating of mucus, and seasonings like pepper, dry mustard and the like cannot injure the delicate membranes.

The best way to use seasonings is to buy them whole, store them in airtight containers, and grind them up only when you're ready to use them. In practice, however, most people will find it more convenient to buy the little cans or bottles of spices and seasonings available at all supermarkets. Companies like Schilling and Spice Islands put out lines of seasonings that include virtually everything the average person will need. Some of these cost a dollar or two, but they can be expected to last as long as two years, so the actual expense is quite small.

Of course, acquiring all the spices and seasonings you will eventually need doesn't have to be done overnight. I just counted how many different jars and bottles I have in my own spice cabinet and I came up with more than 50. But I bought most of these a few at a time.

I started with the basics, including:

salt
pepper
garlic powder*

paprika
parsley
wine vinegar
red and white wine
onion powder/flakes*
soy sauce
Worcestershire sauce

(*Fresh garlic and onions taste much better, but are a little less convenient. However, if you have the time, real garlic and onions are worth the trouble.)

Then, whenever a recipe called for some other seasoning, I would buy it and add it to my collection. By following recipes in this way, I did not have to know what spice to use where. I could just let the author of the recipe tell me. After a while, I began to understand how many of these seasonings should be used.

Along with these commercial seasonings, don't overlook the benefits of garlic, onions and green peppers. Garlic and onions contain a strong germicide, acrolein, which sterilizes the mouth and can help prevent tooth decay. Fresh peppers not only add flavor to food, but are also a good source of Vitamin C.

When you experiment with spices, seasonings and flavorings, you're better off to use too little rather than too much. If you don't add quite enough, no real harm is done. Too much, and the dish can be ruined. Often, just a small amount of some seasoning will be enough to make the food taste great. And don't fall into the trap of thinking that more is necessarily better. One or two spices added to a dish may contribute more to taste than four or five that conflict with each other.

As I've said, the best way to get into using seasonings is to try new recipes and follow the instructions. If you like eggs in the morning, check a bookstore or the library for a cookbook that shows you new and different ways of preparing omelettes and other egg dishes.

But, remember, if you're cooking with spices and seasonings that are unfamiliar to you, you're not necessarily going to love them at first bite. Some of them take a little getting used to, like learning to appreciate a new form of music.

If you're training for competition, or just trying to control your weight, the expert use of seasonings and spices can change a monotonous, restricted diet into an exciting and satisfying one. And you may find there's another advantage as well. When you eat food that's well prepared and seasoned, there's less tendency to bolt down

the meal. We often eat really tasty food more slowly, chew it more, and get more satisfaction from each mouthful. With this kind of meal, the sensation of eating can be so pleasant that there is no need to eat large amounts. Quality takes precedence over quantity, and that makes it a lot easier to stay on a calorie-restricted diet.

As a reference, I am including a partial guide for using herbs, spices, seeds and other seasonings. You may want to do some experimenting on your own, and this reference should give you a head start. As a matter of general practice, the seasonings should be prepared in the following ways:

Seeds and peppercorns—Crushed with a hammer.
Fresh herbs—Minced with scissors or mashed thoroughly with fingertips.
Dried herbs—Pulverized by rolling them between the palms of the hands.

A GUIDE TO SEASONINGS

Beef: savory, basil, marjoram, rosemary; oregano if tomatoes and fresh peppers are also used.

Bread: butter-flavoring; poppy, cardamom, anise, caraway, sesame and cumin seeds; mix in the dough or moisten top of loaf and press seeds into it; rosemary, parsley and other herbs may be added to biscuits and muffins.

Butter-flavoring: add to shortening to be used in making breads, cakes, pastry, and cream sauce, or for sauteing or French frying; measure accurately with a medicine dropper 10 drops of butter-flavoring to 1 cup of oil or soft, warmed shortening; beat into shortening with an egg beater.

Capers: fish, fish cocktails, lamb, mutton, cold tongue, heart; potato salad, tossed salads.

Cheese, American: fresh basil, chives, sage, caraway seeds, dill stalk or dill sauce; add to shredded or grated cheese, moistened to make a paste.

Cheese, cottage: Chinese garlic, chives, fresh basil, dill, parsley, burnet; caraway seeds; multiplying onions or shallots.

Cheese, Swiss: cumin, caraway, sesame, dill or cardamom seeds; dill sauce; basil, chives or sage for spreads.

Chicken gravy and stuffing: savory, tarragon, basil, chives, thyme, marjoram, parsley, sage or rosemary for gravy; all except chives, basil and tarragon for stuffing.

Cookies: anise, cumin, caraway, poppy, sesame and cardamom seeds.

Eggs: Chinese garlic, capers, chives, basil, savory, tarragon, thyme, multiplying-onion tops, or dill sauce; if dried herbs are used, they should be added to the milk to be used in preparing scrambled eggs or omelettes, or to the mayonnaise used in preparing deviled eggs.

Fish: capers, fresh fennel, marjoram, thyme, basil, fresh dill or dill sauce; crushed fennel, dill or anise seeds.

Fruit: rose or mint geranium added to applesauce and discarded after steeping; fresh fennel, mint, and lemon balm for fruit salads; cumin, caraway or anise seeds in applesauce; caraway seeds served with raw apples.

Italian dishes: savory, oregano, basil, rosemary, marjoram, thyme, bay; cumin seeds.

Lamb gravy, sauces, and stuffing: capers, rosemary, savory, chervil, marjoram, fresh dill or dill sauce, mint for sauce.

Pork gravy and stuffing: savory, basil, sage, thyme, chives, Chinese garlic, multiplying-onion tops, parsley; smoke-flavoring for gravy.

Potato salad: fresh dill, dill seeds, dill sauce, caraway seeds, capers.

Rabbit gravy and stuffing: capers, savory, basil, thyme, marjoram, parsley, chives.

Soups and stews: savory, thyme, basil, marjoram, rosemary, chervil, oregano, parsley; grated lemon rind; smoke-flavoring for bean, lentil and split-pea soups; anise, fennel and dill seeds for fish bisques.

Spanish dishes: oregano and marjoram; fresh large and small chilies; chili tepines; cumin and coriander seeds.

Veal gravy and stuffing: marjoram, savory, rosemary, basil.

Vegetable-juice cocktails: basil, marjoram, oregano, tarragon, thyme, savory, chives, Chinese garlic, multiplying-onion tops, parsley.

Vegetables, cooked: fresh dill with potato salad; a tiny amount of mint with peas, carrots or new potatoes; chives with potatoes, string beans and steamed celery root; basil with tomatoes prepared in any manner; oregano with dried beans, lentils, and vegetable dishes with onions and peppers as seasoning; mustard seed with green beans; curry powder or smoke-flavoring with lentils or soybeans; basil or savory with zucchini and summer squash; smoke-flavoring with beans and dry peas.

Vegetable salad: every variety of seed or fresh herb may be added to salad vegetables; dried herbs should be steeped in vinegar to be used for salad dressings.

Sugar and Salt:
What They Do to Your Health and Muscular Development

by Joe Weider

One of the chief reasons that bodybuilders have improved so dramatically over the past few years is better nutrition. There is less bulking up, more careful calorie counting and protein, carbohydrate and fat balance. Vitamin and mineral supplementation insures no lack of these essential elements. But there is a large gulf between nutritional theory and putting food on the table. It isn't enough to know what you *should* be eating. You also have to know how to shop for food and how to prepare it.

That's what this article is about. There are so many more contests than there used to be that bodybuilders have to stay in shape all year long, not just peak once or twice. Eating nothing but tuna fish for 12 months is not only bad for your health, it's also boring. Bodybuilders, like anybody else, need variety in their diet. Moreover, they need to know how to choose foods high in the elements they require and how not to ruin nutritional value in cooking and preparation.

The hardest part of following a healthy, balanced diet is breaking the eating habits you were raised with. You may be able to give up anything for a strict six-week diet, but the trick is to learn new eating patterns that you will maintain the rest of the time. When you try to give up certain kinds of food that you have become accustomed to, it can sometimes be as

traumatic as curing an addiction. Indeed, certain substances you have a habit of ingesting act almost like drugs in your system.

Take sugar and salt, for example. No top bodybuilder would indulge in much of either during a strict diet, but what about the rest of the time? Sure, we are told by nutritionists that sugar represents empty calories—and the fat that follows—and that salt makes you retain water, which makes it difficult to get cut up. But even though these substances are implicated in more serious medical problems, most find it difficult to give them up entirely. In fact, that would probably be hard to do, because sugar and salt are hidden in so many of the foods we eat.

The addiction to sugar and salt begins early in infancy. You may have had little reason to taste commercial baby food lately but, if you have, you know that it tastes pretty good. The manufacturers have realized that babies don't buy baby food, parents do. So in order to sell the product, it is the parents' taste buds that have to be tickled. Baby food is usually loaded with sugar and salt, substances adults are accustomed to. Unfortunately, this teaches children to expect food to taste overly sweet or salty, and their addiction is begun.

Salt was originally used as a preservative. It was so valuable, it was frequently used as money. We get sodium and chloride—the constituents of

table salt—naturally in the foods we eat without having to add any from a salt shaker. However, between the extra salt we sprinkle on our food and the amounts added by food processors, we end up with 10 to 25 times too much.

Bodybuilders, as we've mentioned, already know that salt causes fluid retention in the body. Obviously, a bloated, puffy physique is not going to win contests. But salt is also implicated in hypertension, a disease that can kill you before you even know you have it. Cutting back on salt is made more difficult by the fact that manufacturers of adult food products, just like those who make the baby food, try to make it more palatable by adding lots of salt. Even if you throw away your salt shaker—which you should—you still may be getting too much salt.

The balance between sodium and potassium in your body is very important. Processed foods frequently lead to an imbalance of these elements. The closer you get to natural foods— fresh vegetables and fruits instead of convenience foods—the better is your chance of maintaining this balance. Instead of salt on the table, you can season food with pepper, paprika, thyme, curry, garlic and dry mustard. Also, substitute garlic and onion *powder* for garlic and onion *salt*.

Bodybuilders also try to stay away from sugar when they are dieting. The sugar we are talking about is sucrose, the manmade kind found in the sugar bowl. Actually, as opposed to the antiquity of salt usage, processed sugar only became common in the diet about 100 years ago. Americans en masse suddenly started using it in every conceivable food preparation.

There are other kinds of sugars. *Fructose* comes from fruits and vegetables; *lactose* from milk; and *glucose* is a form of sugar found in the bloodstream. These are important and nutritionally valuable forms of food. But processed sugar is nothing but empty calories, likely to do nothing for the body but add to the level of fat storage. A bodybuilder who indulges in eating too much sugar—whether from the bowl, in cakes, cookies and soft drinks, or even hidden in commercial hamburgers—is just not doing himself any good. And honey, frequently used as a sugar substitute, is even worse. It is actually many times sweeter than processed sugar.

With the rise in sugar usage came increased cavities and tooth decay. And even more

significant, a rise in the incidence of diabetes. The link between excessive sugar use and diabetes is certain, and that alone should discourage its use. Additionally, high levels of sugar in the body seem to have an adverse effect on the liver. Bodybuilders taking anabolics, who cannot afford to put any extra stress on the liver, should take note.

Sugar is thought of as an energy food. In fact, it takes several hours for the body to break down and use this energy, so there is no immediate lift. And sugar in excess can actually work like a depressant on the body. It makes a lot more sense, if you have a sweet tooth, to satisfy it with fruit instead. Add spices like fennel and cinnamon to the dishes you prepare. These will give you an interesting and exotic taste experience, and you won't miss the sugar.

Above all, make an effort to avoid the sugar that manufacturers and restaurants have hidden in the food they serve. The number of items which contain sugar is incredible. For instance, out of the entire variety of breakfast cereals carried by one Los Angeles supermarket, only one was completely sugar-free. Check labels on the products you buy. Buy fresh foods and prepare them yourself, rather than heating up something pre-packaged or patronizing a fast-food stand.

Sugar is like a drug, and you can experience withdrawal when you cut it out of your diet. It isn't easy. So when you get a sudden craving for gum, hot dogs, hamburgers, ketchup, soup or even cough medicine, it may be that your body wants a "fix" from the sugar contained in these products.

One last thing: some people are trying to cut out sugar by switching to saccharin and the products that contain it. A Canadian study found that saccharin is carcinogenic—that is, it causes cancer. This fact is often ignored, since the popular myth is that these findings are not valid due to the huge doses of saccharin given the test animals. Unfortunately, this is not true.

Something is either a carcinogen, or it isn't. When you are given large doses of a carcinogen, it merely increases the statistical incidence of cancer and speeds up the testing process. Saccharin was found to cause cancer and to be especially dangerous to men. Until a legitimate scientific study contradicts these findings, anyone who uses saccharin, just like anybody who smokes, is running a risk.

Fruit:
Nature's Dessert

by Joe Weider

"I was fat as a kid," one top bodybuilder revealed recently, "and so I have a lot of fat cells. This means that when I'm getting ready for a contest, I have to keep to a very strict diet. If it wasn't for fruit, I'd go crazy."

You can see his point. Fruit is nature's own dessert. It contains the three basic kinds of sugars—fructose, glucose and sucrose—and is relatively high in bulk and low in calories. Fruit generally contains next to no fat, and is high in such vitamins as C or A. All of this makes fruit a natural for a bodybuilder who needs to keep up his energy level but wants to stay cut up.

However, just as with vegetables, it's pretty easy to mistreat fruit and end up robbing it of much of its nutritional value. For instance, enzyme action in many fruits results in excessive vitamin loss. This enzyme action is accelerated by warm temperatures, the exposure of the fruit to both oxygen and light, and by contact with copper or iron. If fruits are to be cooked, the cooking should be done very rapidly to minimize the enzyme action.

While the vitamin content of fruit continues to increase until the fruit is ripe, overripe fruit left at room temperature begins to lose vitamins A, B_2 and C almost immediately. That's why it's best to eat ripe fruit as soon as possible, or put it into the refrigerator. An exception to this refrigeration rule is fruit that has a heavy peel, such as apples, oranges and bananas. As the Chiquita Banana people always tell us, you don't have to refrigerate these types of fruit.

Exposure to oxygen increases the loss of Vitamin C. This means that no fruit should be cut or peeled until just before you are going to eat it. Soft fruits, like grapes or berries, should be kept in the refrigerator, unwashed and unstemmed. Even small amounts of handling can cause bruises in these fruits and that leads to increased enzyme action, which destroys vitamins.

Don't place fruits in prolonged contact with water. Fruits should never be soaked. This causes vitamins C and B and sugars to dissolve out and be lost. Instead, wash fruits quickly. If you are trying to remove the skin from peaches, don't soak them in hot water, steam them. After only brief exposure to steam, the skin comes right off.

When cutting apples, you can avoid the

discoloration that sometimes occurs by chilling the apples first, and being careful not to use a knife that contains copper. This discoloration is not just a cosmetic change. It indicates a complete loss of Vitamin C in the discolored areas. Since acid retards the enzyme activity that destroys vitamins, a little lemon juice mixed in with the cut fruit will prevent this vitamin loss. Incidentally, when a fruit has an edible peel, you would do well to eat the peel. If not, you deprive yourself of a good deal of the fruit's nutritional value.

By and large, the more you process, juice, squeeze or otherwise alter fruit from its raw, natural state, the less you end up getting in nutritional value. This means that oranges are better for you than orange juice, and apples have more nutritional value than apple juice or apple sauce.

If you decide not to eat fruit raw and plain, there are more effective and less effective ways to proceed from there. For instance, you should keep oranges in the refrigerator until they are chilled before you try to extract the juice. Then, extract the juice quickly to avoid prolonged exposure to air. It also makes a difference whether you are planning to drink the juice immediately or not. Fermentation and oil from the skin are responsible for that bitter taste after orange juice has been standing for a while. So you should squeeze the oranges lightly, being careful not to extract much oil from the skin, if you plan to keep the juice in the refrigerator for any length of time.

Since exposure to air destroys Vitamin C, orange juice which is kept in the refrigerator will lose a lot of its Vitamin C unless you store it in a closed container that's so full there's almost no oxygen inside. And as you use up the juice, you have to continue to transfer it to smaller containers. This is so much trouble that it makes sense to only squeeze the juice you are going to use at that particular time. Another advantage of this is that it takes time, and anything you can do to make meal preparation more time-consuming will tend to keep you from gulping down too many calories.

All of the above may seem to be much ado about nothing, unless you realize that if the procedures we've recommended are not followed, orange juice can lose as much as 50% of its Vitamin C content *in a single hour!* And what, after all, are you drinking the orange juice for if not for that Vitamin C? Well, Vitamin A, of course, but you can ruin that pretty easily as well.

Cooking helps destroy the enzymes which cause vitamin loss. This means that juices that have been cooked, such as canned tomato or grapefruit juice, are able to retain their vitamin content more effectively than fresh juices. Also, although Vitamin C is one of the most easily destroyed vitamins, synthetic Vitamin C, containing no enzymes, is extremely durable. Therefore, if you are not going to consume the juice immediately (in other words, if prolonged storage will be involved), it sometimes makes more sense to use concoctions with Vitamin C added.

Actually, fruits don't lose much of their nutritional value when they're frozen. Therefore, having some frozen fruit in your freezer is not a bad idea. However, you should follow two rules: be sure that no sweeteners (sugar, corn syrup or the like) have been added, and use the product immediately after defrosting.

The problem with juicing or processing fruits, aside from any nutritional loss, is that you tend to increase the caloric content of what you're eating. Compare, for instance, oranges and orange juice in terms of calories, carbohydrates and vitamins:

	One Orange	One Cup Orange Juice
Calories	65	110
Carbs	16 g	26 g
Vitamin A	260 I.U.	500 I.U.
Vitamin C	66 mg	124 mg

This comparison shows that you almost double all of the values for oranges when you transform them into orange juice. This is obviously due to the higher concentration: it takes more than one orange to make a cup of orange juice. The higher values for C and A are fine, but look at the increase in calories and carbs. Also, remember that this is for *one cup.* I remember one individual in the gym who kept complaining that he couldn't lose weight. He then admitted that he drank at least a quart of orange juice a day. You figure it out.

Incorporating fruit into your menu is not difficult. Some juice with breakfast, an apple or pear with lunch, and maybe a fruit salad with dinner can add a great deal of variety and enjoyment to your meals. Or if you're looking for yet another way to serve fruit, try one of the following recipes:

Remove cores and cut chilled red apples into ½-inch-thick slices. Spread slices with cream cheese, and sprinkle with caraway or poppy seeds.

Or . . .

Cut a cantaloupe or other small melon in half, making sawtooth edges. Remove seeds. Cut thin slice from bottom of each half so that it will rest securely on plate. Fill center with one of the following:
—*diced pineapple, sliced peaches or other fruit*
—*unstemmed black cherries*
—*strawberries*
—*mixed diced fruits*
—*mixture of diced fruit and plain, low-fat yogurt, or fruit and unsweetened gelatin*

With a little thought, you can come up with a thousand ways of serving fruit, or mixing it with any number of other delicious foods that will still keep you on a reasonable diet. But all fruits are not alike, and sometimes you can be surprised when you think you are getting one thing and you end up with quite another.

Strawberries, for example, are so sweet and tasty that it would seem foolhardy to include them in your diet if you're trying to get cut up. But a cup of strawberries only contains 55 calories and 13 grams of carbohydrates. Likewise, half a cantaloupe contains a mere 60 calories and 14 grams of carbohydrates. Obviously, neither fruit is harmful to a diet.

One banana, on the other hand, contains 100 calories and 26 grams of carbohydrate, a good deal more than the above two fruits but still not prohibitive. But then we come to a fruit that is extremely popular in California and elsewhere, the avocado. Delicious, but a problem.

As I said earlier, more fruits contain little or no fat, but not so the avocado. One avocado contains about 37 grams of fat! As a result, you are getting about 370 calories when you eat a medium-sized avocado, and too much fat to really stay cut up. Thankfully, this is one of the few examples of a wolf-in-sheep's-clothing you get with fruit.

One bit of information about fruit as part of a balanced diet: fruit is virtually pure carbohydrate. It contains, as a rule, little or no fat or protein.

While a balanced diet is essential for satisfying appetite and maintaining energy levels, too many carbs in the diet can be as much of a problem as too few. Therefore, it may be ill-advised to have a fruit dessert with a meal containing a lot of vegetables, potatoes or rice. Carbohydrates are primarily an energy food, and once you have satisfied your body's need for fuel, excess carbohydrate calories are just going to create fat deposits.

One way to maintain this necessary balance in your diet is to combine fruit with protein foods, such as yogurt or cottage cheese. Generations of dieters have found that almost any fruit goes well with cottage cheese, or with yogurt. Courtesy of Adelle Davis, you might want to try:

Raspberry Yogurt

Shake or beat until smooth:
   1 cup chilled juice from canned raspberries, and
   ⅓ cup powdered milk.
Add and beat slightly:
   1 cup yogurt.
Pour into chilled glasses and serve.

Make fruit a major part of your diet, but also take care to get the most out of the fruit you eat.

Snacks:

The Pauses That Refresh

by Bill Dobbins

"Snack" sounds like some kind of modern, made-up word, but it really has ancient origins. It probably comes from an old Flemish word meaning "a quick snap or bite," like the kind delivered by an angry dog. The word was used in that sense as early as 1402, but it was first used in the modern sense about the middle of the 18th century.

The snack, as in "a mere bite or morsel of food, as contrasted with a regular meal; a light or incidental repast," has taken on a new meaning in these days of convenience foods and sedentary, stressful lifestyles. The snack today is less likely to be a "light repast" as it is a plateful of Hostess Twinkies.

However, bodybuilders attempting to stay in or near contest shape cannot afford the luxury of high-sugar desserts. But while most of them are aware of the problems that between-meal eating can cause, they get hungry just like anybody else.

Then there is the would-be bodybuilder, the teenager who has just started training and is dreaming of becoming Mr. Universe, but unfortunately he still has the eating habits of Fat Albert. For youngsters like these, it's not easy to give up the cake, cookies and other sweet snacks

that their growing adolescent bodies have been able to burn off until now.

Thus, for beginner and advanced bodybuilder alike, it's important to learn how to incorporate the right between-meal eating habits into the training regimen. And the right habits involve:

1. Knowing how to balance snacks with regular meals.

2. Knowing what kinds of foods to snack on.

The first thing to recognize is that food is food, whether it's eaten in regular meals or snacks. The food you snack on contributes to your total nutritional picture or detracts from it in the same way as the food you eat at mealtime. Furthermore, those between-meal calories become part of your total energy intake and can result in fat level increases if you eat too much.

But it's also true that a number of small meals are easier to digest than one big one. Eating the right kind of snacks, or "light repasts," means you spread out your nutritional and caloric intake over a longer period of time, thus benefiting both your health and physique.

This kind of light meal should be easy to prepare. Perhaps you may want to have it prepared in advance. Salads are an obvious choice, and they can be an excellent source of

46

nutrition. One way to have salads available instantly is to get a bunch of small plastic containers with tight lids and make your own salad bar. The basics for this kind of salad bar would include:

lettuce	mushrooms
tomatoes	artichoke hearts
cucumbers	seed sprouts
pickles	green onions
radishes	celery
	coleslaw

To provide vitamin and mineral content, you can add the following raw vegetables:

broccoli	cauliflower
carrots	spinach

Cooked asparagus spears are also a delicious addition.

To give you a source of protein, include the following items in your salad bar:

chicken	hard-boiled eggs
(and other fowl)	cooked fish
tuna	cold meats
	cottage cheese

Obviously, a salad with all or most of these ingredients could easily grow into quite a meal! The trick is to include a limited and different selection of ingredients in each snack to give you variety and to keep the calories low.

Also, if you don't want to go to the trouble of making a salad, most of the protein sources listed above make excellent snacks all by themselves. Certainly, cooking a lot of extra chicken and having it handy in the refrigerator gives you a quick, healthy, high-protein goodie whenever you want it.

Vegetables also make good snacks. Munching on a carrot or a stalk of celegy gives you the feeling of eating without the risk of putting on fat. If celery doesn't sound appetizing enough, try eating it with a little sour cream dip—just a little. That should do the trick!

As nutritious as the above suggestions may be, many people still cannot think of snacks without picturing something sweet. The answer to their craving is fruit, nature's own dessert. Fructose, which accounts for the sweet taste of fruit, is many times sweeter than table sugar. However, it's present in such relatively small amounts that fruit is low in calories (but high in vitamins and minerals).

You can eat various fruits individually. Or you can cut them up to make a fruit salad. Pour a little lemon juice over the cut-up fruit to pick up the taste even more, and serve with cottage cheese if you want to obtain some protein value.

Strawberries and cream is an excellent and simple dessert which also makes a great snack. Remember, the cream contains a lot of fat, so go easy on it. But its natural sweetness complements that of the strawberries.

Another food that goes well with fruit is yogurt. Avoid those prepackaged yogurt and fruit mixes. They are full of sugar and enormously high in calories. But unsweetened low-fat yogurt combined with a fruit of your choice makes a tasty, nutritious snack and it's simple to prepare. In fact, if you are ambitious enough, you might try making your own yogurt by using one of the many appliances specifically designed for this task.

Nowadays there are many diet-snack products on the market to take the place of sugar, candy and cake. Ingredients such as granola, soy powder and whole wheat flour are used in these products. These diet snacks are available from health food stores, or you can make your own if you wish. For example, try this recipe:

Protein Logs

4 cups tofu (soy bean curd)
½ cup powdered soy milk or carob
3 cups natural peanut butter
1 cup barley/corn malt or sorghum syrup
Sesame seeds or coconut

Mix ingredients together and form into four or five logs. Roll in sesame seeds or coconut for added crunch. Refrigerate on wax paper. Slice to serve.

If this kind of snack appeals to you, you'll find many more recipes like this in cookbooks that are available at bookstores and health food stores.

These are just a few suggestions for snacks to get you through from one meal to another. Going hungry is not the answer to maintaining weight or providing your body with the proper nutrition. When you get to mealtime and you're starved, you're more likely to overeat, and that doesn't do you any good at all.

Keep in mind the effect of sweets on your system. A dose of sugar hits your bloodstream and raises your blood sugar level tremendously. Your body immediately releases a lot of insulin to cope with all this additional glucose. This makes your blood sugar level plummet once more—and you get hungry.

One common bodybuilding practice is to eat six meals per day—three small meals and three snacks, all spaced 2–3 hours apart during the day. To maintain your body weight, these six meals should total 3500 calories per day. To lose weight at a rate of one pound per week, your meals should total 3000 calories per day.

To gain weight on a six-meals-per-day nutrition schedule, you should increase the caloric total of each of your snacks, being sure that each snack is high in protein. A great snack for weight-gainers is a shake made from a half cup of Weider Crash Weight Gain powder, a pint of raw whole milk, and a scoop of ice cream or piece of fruit (bananas and strawberries are best). Mix these ingredients in your blender and have the shake as one of your snacks. You'll notice a positive weight-gain cycle developing after only 3–5 days on the above eating schedule.

In closing, I'd like to leave you with one more idea, a simple, often overlooked snack that's one of my favorites—cereal and nonfat milk. You may have to search carefully through your supermarket shelves to find a modern cereal that is not loaded with sugar, but they do exist. If some shredded wheat, milk and perhaps some strawberries or banana slices isn't tasty enough for you, maybe you had better go back to the Twinkies and Ho Hos and forget about bodybuilding.

Getting into Soups

by Bill Dobbins

Bodybuilders on pre-contest diets all face the same problem: to get cut up, you need to cut down on calories; but when you limit your caloric intake, you can rob yourself of needed vitamins and minerals.

A way around this difficulty is to eat soups—not the kind you buy in cans, but ones made at home. Soups provide a method of concentrating vitamins and minerals while keeping calories to a minimum. They can also be an excellent source of protein. So a properly prepared soup dish is a completely balanced meal in itself.

Soups should be made in two stages. First, there is the stock, made well in advance, if that suits you, from leftovers, bones and table scraps. Then there's the soup itself, a combination of the stock and a variety of fresh, wholesome ingredients.

To begin, you need to save all your vegetable parings—outer leaves of lettuce, cabbage, spinach, chard, kale and parsley; bits of tomato, celery stalks, asparagus, the tops of green onions, the peelings of squash, beets, turnips, cucumbers, rutabagas and so on. Any part of any vegetable, as long as it is not actually spoiled or decaying, should be put in a plastic bag and kept in the refrigerator.

Next, save and put aside meat scraps and all bones, no matter what kind. These should also be kept in the refrigerator, preferably next to the freezing unit. If you have a really big bone (e.g., a ham or a turkey bone), you should use it within 24 hours to make soup stock.

Bones are an important part of soup making since they provide such a good array of minerals. The more bone surface that's exposed to the liquid, the more minerals are obtained, so it's a good idea to cut, break or saw the bones into pieces that are as small as possible. Doing this will also add to the flavor.

Searing the bone pieces is essential to break down the protein and to improve the flavor, especially when you use fresh bones that still have meat attached. Be careful not to char the meat scraps.

To get the calcium from the bones, add vinegar to the cooking water. Also add a bit of salt, since this helps to draw out the juices from the bones and meat scraps.

The vegetables should be thoroughly chopped, since this allows more of the flavor and nutrients to pass into the stock. Normally, when you cook vegetables you try not to let their vitamin and mineral content get washed out, but that is exactly what you do when you make soup stock. Of course, in this case the vitamins and minerals will remain in the stock, which is why soups are so high in nutrition.

After you chop up the vegetables, boil them for 15 minutes and then let them stand and soak to permit their nutrients to pass into the water. When you've finished cooking your stock, pour it through a cloth to trap the bits of bone and the vegetable fiber. You now have a quantity of soup stock that can be used right away or frozen for use later.

When the stock cools off, the fat will rise to the top. Skim this off. You can also add a little salt and pepper, some cayenne or a chili pepper for flavor. Now you can go on to prepare the soup, or simply use the soup stock itself as bouillon.

A bouillon is a variation of seasoned soup stock. Just heat, season to taste, and serve. A consomme is another variation, made from bones rather than a combination of ingredients. Consommes are extremely rich in minerals but have few calories, and this makes them ideal for dieting bodybuilders. Here is one suggestion for a good-tasting beef consomme that is easy to prepare.

Beef Consomme

Using assorted beef bones, make one quart of stock. Remove the fat, reheat the stock and add the following:

1 small clove garlic
1 pinch each of marjoram, thyme and basil
1 to 2 tablespoons minced chives or tops of green onions
1 to 3 drops Tabasco

Stir well, and simmer for 10 minutes. Remove garlic, taste for seasoning, and garnish with thin slices of lemon, topped with a dash of paprika.

When you use vegetables to make soup, don't soak them or cook them too long or you'll destroy both their taste and nutritional value.

Vegetable Soup

Dice or shred the following chilled vegetables, and saute them in fat from stock:

2 carrots
1 or 2 onions or leeks
2 or 3 stalks celery
1 unpeeled potato

Add:
¼ teaspoon crushed black peppercorns
¼ crushed bay leaf
Pinch each of basil, marjoram and savory

Cover utensil, keep heat moderate, and do not brown. When vegetables are tender, add and heat quickly:

1 quart soup stock
¼ cup soy or peanut flour
1 teaspoon salt
2 tablespoons parsley

Serve when hot.

Using soy or peanut flour adds protein to the

soup. Another way to boost protein content, although it also adds some calories, is to use ground meat.

Vegetable Soup with Ground Meat

Combine and heat in soup kettle:
1 to 2 tablespoons fat from stock
1 minced clove garlic
1 or 2 chopped onions
2 chopped stalks celery
2 chilled diced carrots
1 chilled, unpeeled, diced potato

Cover the utensil. Keep heat high for a short time until vegetables are heated, then lower temperature and cook for about 10 minutes until they are tender. Add and heat quickly:

2 quarts soup stock
2 teaspoons salt
¼ crushed bay leaf
½ teaspoon crushed black peppercorns
Pinch each marjoram, thyme and savory

Simmer stock 10 minutes. Add and stir rapidly:

1 lb. finely ground beef
2 tablespoons ground parsley

Taste for seasoning. Serve immediately without further heating.

When you add ground beef to soup like this, it cooks almost immediately, so there is no reason to leave it over the heat for any length of time.

Humans have no doubt been making soups since the discovery of fire, and there is no shortage of soup recipes in any good cookbook. You can make chowders from fish, cream soups abounding in protein and calcium, and bean soup, chili soup, tomato soup, etc. The time-consuming part of the process is making the stock. Once you have this, you can whip together a soup in no time.

Soups are as economical as they are nutritious. Since they are made from leftovers and food you would normally throw away, or bones purchased at a butcher shop, the cost can be negligible.

Including soup in your menu is like taking an excellent vitamin/mineral supplement in savory form. You get a lot of nutrition and very few calories. How can you beat that?

Cutting Up with a Low-Fat Diet:

How to Keep Up Your Protein Intake without Loading Your Body with Unnecessary Calories

by Bill Dobbins

Most bodybuilders would agree that diet is very important in preparing a contest-ready physique, and that a high intake of protein is an essential part of that diet. However, a problem with high-protein diets is that they also tend to be high in fat, and, therefore, calories. Since body fat can only be reduced by burning more calories than you take in, it is a waste of time and energy taking in more calories than you need while you are trying to cut up.

Meat is a good source of complete protein, and bodybuilders eat a lot of it. But animal protein also contains a good deal of fat. For example, 75% of the calories in beef come from the fat it contains—a three-ounce steak provides 20 grams of protein, but 27 grams of fat as well. Bodybuilders are generally aware of this, and switch to chicken or fish to get ready for contests, but even then they may be inadvertently including hidden amounts of fat in their meals.

Chicken is a favorite food of bodybuilders in training. Looking at the numbers, you can see why. A cooked chicken breast of 3.3 ounces provides 25 grams of protein, and only five grams of fat. Because it is so low in fat, chicken breast contains only 155 calories, as opposed to the 330 calories you would get in the steak.

More protein, fewer calories and less fat are good reasons to prefer chicken over beef.

Chicken, of course, can be ruined as a food for bodybuilders by the way it is prepared. For example, if you think the stuff that the Colonel sells bears any resemblance to the chicken breast you cook in your oven, you would also probably buy land in Nevada from a used car salesman. The kind of chicken you get at most fast-food places is saturated with fat from deep-frying, and it's coated with starch. This can easily double or triple the number of calories, and add a lot of carbohydrates as well.

Chicken in other dishes can be a problem, too. An eight-ounce chicken pot pie contains about 535 calories and has more than 30 grams of fat. While this is a nutritious enough food, a bodybuilder should be concerned about keeping his fat intake down to about 30% of his diet. This takes a bit of effort when you're on a high-protein diet. Avoiding fat-loaded dishes is one way to do this, but knowing how to treat the foods you eat is another.

For example, take a close look at a piece of chicken before you cook it next time. Take hold of the skin and pull some of it loose. The skin of chicken looks so crisp and inviting after it has been cooked, but when it's raw you can see it is

nothing but fat, and about as appetizing as blubber. So just tear it off, and feed it to the dog, throw it away, or whatever. Put some paprika on the chicken before you cook it and it will come out looking just as crisp as if the skin were still on it.

Oil is another source of calories and fat. A tablespoon of vegetable oil contains about 125 calories and 14 grams of fat. Anything you fry in oil picks up some of those calories and some of the fat. Therefore, as most bodybuilders are aware, it pays to broil or roast meat rather than fry it. But there are other ways to cut back on your intake of oil. Use a low-cal salad dressing instead of one that uses salad oil. Sure, you will get more carbs this way, but you won't get the calories and the extra fat. And be aware: Margarine affects your diet in the same way as vegetable oil. Unless you go to a low-cal butter substitute, you are still getting hundreds of extra calories and many grams of fat.

One whole egg contains 80 calories, six grams of protein and six grams of fat. That makes it an almost ideal food for bodybuilders. However, as contest time rolls around, you can go it even one better by eating the white of the egg only. This gives you only about 20% of the calories and virtually none of the fat, while still providing two-thirds of the protein.

Fish is also popular with bodybuilders because of its protein content and relatively low amount of fat. Obviously, you have to cook it properly and avoid adding breading and oil in order to preserve its low fat level. But many people do not know the tricks for cooking fish properly. These are worth going into, because some of them apply to other meats as well.

First of all, all meat (or fish) contains some fat. When it is cooked, this fat tends to turn liquid. Therefore, it is best to have the meat sitting up on a rack so that the fats and oils can drip down and not stay in the food. Whether broiling or roasting, use some sort of rack to allow this to happen. And when you remove the food from the oven, pat it dry with paper towels in the same way you would in the case of french fries. This applies to beef, chicken, fish, etc. Look at how much liquid clings to the paper. Remember: Grease is worth about 125 calories a tablespoon!

With fish, it is generally best to cook it as little as possible. Above a certain temperature, the oils remaining in the fish are affected and you get that "fishy" taste and smell. Thin fillets of fish, like whitefish or perch, need only to be cooked on one side in the broiler, and then only to a temperature of about 140 degrees. Thicker fish, like trout, will need to be cooked on both sides.

Tuna is also a favorite of bodybuilders. For convenience sake, a lot of bodybuilders eat the kind packed in cans—and in oil. It is not enough just to drain this oil out of the can. A lot of it stays with the tuna. Instead, take the tuna out of the can and wrap it in a paper towel. Get as much of the oil out of it as you can. Then put the tuna in some sort of plastic container if you are not planning to finish it in one sitting. Bear in mind also that adding mayonnaise to the tuna is putting calories back in at a rate of 100 per tablespoon.

Most bodybuilders avoid milk and cheese products before a contest because they feel these foods make them smooth. They are probably right. A cup of whole milk contains 160 calories and nine grams of fat along with the nine grams of protein it provides. If you switch to low-fat milk, you only get 145 calories and five grams of fat. But if you drink *nonfat* milk, your caloric intake is 50% less, and you get no fat at all. Meanwhile, the amount of protein per volume actually increases! This makes milk in this form compatible with most bodybuilders' diets.

Some "diet" products are suitable for bodybuilders and some are not. You just have to learn to read labels. A diet salad dressing that has little fat but enormous amounts of calories is no bargain. Also, some low-cal foods contain only a third or so less calories but may also provide fewer grams of protein, lack vitamins, and cost a fortune. There are a lot of gullible people out there trying to lose weight.

Obviously, you cannot and should not cut fat out of your diet entirely. But you are probably going to get plenty without adding more to your diet unnecessarily. After a certain amount, the fat you eat automatically tends to become fat on your body, and that is no way to win bodybuilding competitions.

There is another way of getting the proper balance of fat in your diet without sacrificing protein. That's by eating less meat and a lot more vegetables. Some vegetables are remarkably high in protein and low in fat. Lacto-vegetarian bodybuilders like Bill Pearl have proved you can develop a championship physique without eating meat at all.

But eating vegetables does you no good unless they are properly prepared, and it is very easy to ruin them by improper handling and cooking.

Fasting for Losing Fat and Regenerating Body Vigor

by Andreas Cahling

Man is a slow learner. Neither nature itself nor irrefutable history seems able to convince him that sometimes *not* eating is healthful. Instead, bodybuilders continue to gorge themselves with every food available and suffer from all sorts of problems as a result (protein overdoses, hypoglycemia, obesity), not to mention that they bring their muscularity quest to a grinding halt.

Yet all the evidence is there. Wild animals are not only able to heal themselves without drugs, but they do not suffer from being overweight. Since creation, nature has been beating us over the head with the fact that animals have always instinctively avoided food while feeling ill. To these "lower" animals, a decreased appetite during disease is an alarm signal, telling them to "starve a fever." Still, we can't seem to grasp that. We continue to flaunt our favorite maxim of conceit: "Man is the only rational animal." Of course, that's man's definition, not animal's.

As if nature weren't qualified enough as a teacher, we've also failed to grasp the message of thousands of years of history. Even before the age of tribal medicine men, fasting was used to cure diseases and rejuvenate the body. Hippocrates, the "Father of Medicine," recommended fasting, while Socrates and Plato used fasting to obtain physical and mental highs. The Greeks were not alone in their respect of

fasting; philosophers and yogis of the Orient—known for longevity and mental acuity, as well as spiritual consciousness—practiced fasting.

The logic behind fasting is convincing. Let's start with Hans Selye, the renowned Canadian physician and author. Selye's concept is basic: A person is as young or old as his smallest vital component—the cell; therefore, to maintain youth and health, our bodies must constantly be producing more new cells to replace dead cells. Unfortunately, when we allow waste products to build up in our bodies, these products interfere with the growth of new cells by inhibiting the transportation of nutrients. To resist aging, we must not only promote the building of new cells, but we must also eliminate aged and dead cells from our bodies as quickly as possible.

SOURCE OF REJUVENATION

Fasting becomes necessary when there is no longer an effective means of rapidly clearing out cellular waste to provide a healthful environment for new cells.

How can something as simple as abstinence from food provide such positive results? During a prolonged fast (more than three days), the body lives on its own tissue. Sounds dangerous for a bodybuilder, doesn't it? Yet, ironically,

55

fasting is probably the most healthful road you can take toward bodybuilding success. Here's why:

The "secret" of fasting's effectiveness is that the body is selective in the use of its own cells. First, to satisfy its nourishment needs, it starts breaking down and burning the cells which are diseased, degenerated, old or dead. During a fast, the body feeds on the most unclean and inferior material in the body, such as fat deposits, tumors, etc. Cells from important body organs, the nervous system and the brain, will not be used. The advantage of this process to the bodybuilder is obvious: with the widespread, stupid use of steroids today and a prepossessing lust for "getting ripped," the fast is a means of achieving new muscle tissue, rejuvenated strength and cells. In this area, I believe it's superior to the most sophisticated diets known.

It's difficult to believe that your body can actually build new cells faster when you limit your nutrients, but it's a physiological fact. Fasting requires a faith in your body's ability to take care of itself. In fact, if you give it a chance, your body will do a better job of maintaining its own health than you can.

Even though no protein is consumed during a fast, your blood protein level will remain normal. That's because the protein in your body will be converted from one form to another in order to satisfy specific needs. Amino acids—the building blocks of protein—can be reused time after time to build new cells.

FAST FOR STRENGTH

Waste products reduce your body's efficiency, so your objective should be to get rid of them as quickly as possible. When you fast, organs such as lungs, kidneys and liver are relieved of their waste loads, freeing them for higher work capacities. That's why you experience renewed energy during a fast. And remember, there's no reason to cut back on your workouts; in fact, you can approach them with renewed vigor.

ATTITUDE TOWARD FASTING

Mental attitude can mean the difference between success and failure during a fast. Just remember that there is no relationship between forced starvation and voluntary abstinence from food. Forced starvation carries with it uncertainty and fear, which has a paralyzing effect on body functions and can damage your health.

However, if you approach fasting with a

Bob Jodkiewicz (left) and the author of this article, Andreas Cahling, two of the world's most muscular men, can speak of fasting from their own experience. "Fasting is great for bodybuilders," says Cahling, "because it helps eliminate aged, dead cells and promotes the building of new ones."

confidence and a full understanding of its benefits, your body, in turn, will respond to this positive attitude.

Even symptoms that seem adverse are actually beneficial results of a fast. For example, after the first two or three days, you might experience a slight headache and light dizziness. Your skin might even break out. But this just means that the amount of toxins expelled during a fast can be 10 times the normal level. Try to ignore your anxiety and be proud of the fast's cleansing effect.

THE RIGHT WAY TO FAST

For optimum bodybuilding benefits, you should go on a short fast about three months before your next contest. This will stimulate your body's natural anabolism for increased muscle tissue production, while bringing out your cuts and giving you new training energy and motivation.

If you have been using steroids or other drugs, their effects may linger after you stop taking

them, so allow about two months for your body to return to normal before undertaking a fast to cleanse it.

Since supplements can only be assimilated in combination with food, they should also be curtailed. During a fast, you would simply be wasting them.

If you've never fasted before, or if you plan on fasting only with water, definitely see your physician first. A fruit and vegetable fast for a limited time, on the other hand, presents no danger and is something that you can begin tomorrow.

Some might claim that a fast on juices rather than water is not a "real" fast, but it's actually the superior one. Juices accelerate the body's cleansing capacity by supplying necessary minerals and ionic charges.

To prepare your body for a fast, begin with a two- or three-day diet consisting of only raw fruit and vegetables as well as juices. Eat fruit one meal and juices the next; do not mix fruit and vegetables at the same meal, because each requires different enzymes for proper digestion.

On the fourth day, begin your juice diet and remain on it for four to six days. Gradually, feelings of hunger will disappear. Drink as much juice as you can—this both increases the cleansing action and subdues hunger. Carrot, celery, apple and watermelon juices are all excellent.

HOW TO STOP FASTING

The famous "health doctor" Otto F. Buchinger said, "Even an idiot can fast, but only a wise man knows how to break a fast." In other words, the great benefits of a fast can be sabotaged if your return to a solid food diet is not done properly.

Here are some important rules for returning to a "normal" diet:

1. Eat small amounts
2. Eat slowly and chew thoroughly
3. *Gradually* return to a normal diet

During this transition period of two or three days, your diet should consist of only raw fruit and vegetables. Then gradually include other foods.

Perhaps the most important rule of all is to completely avoid all coffee and drugs. A fast highly sensitizes your body to drugs, and the smallest amount can seriously damage you.

Try fasting. Your first experience will be an astounding one. The fast will not only change the composition of your body, but also your mind. Rather than maintaining a body composed of diseased cells and painful poisons, you'll have a body consisting of pure, natural organic nutrients and fresh, new muscle tissue. And rather than having a mind of pure, self-limiting ego, you'll have fresh, clear brain power. And that's the *only* way to the top!

Eating on the Road

by Joe Weider

Maintaining your diet and getting proper nutrition is difficult enough when you're preparing food in your own kitchen. But it is even harder when you have to eat out.

When bodybuilders travel to contests, exhibitions or seminars, they have no choice but to eat most of their meals out. Also, I see bodybuilders all the time who have come to Santa Monica to train for a few weeks or months at Gold's or World Gym, and many of them stay in hotels or furnished rooms that have no cooking facilities.

How and what you eat can determine whether or not you will succeed in bodybuilding. When you get up onstage, no judge is going to make allowances for the fact that you haven't been eating home-cooked meals.

Of course, there are really two elements to maintaining your diet while you're on the road—knowing what to eat, and sticking to your diet, no matter what. Without discipline, nutritional knowledge will do you no good.

Traveling with Arnold Schwarzenegger recently, I saw a good example of this kind of discipline. Although Arnold is not in training for competition at present, and even though he outweighs me by something like 50 pounds, I don't think we sat down to a single meal in which he didn't eat less than I did.

On airplanes, Arnold always ignored the bread and dessert that came with the meals. In restaurants, he generally chose fish for lunch, with perhaps some rice on the side. By dinner time, he might indulge in something heavier, and maybe a glass of wine, but he had disciplined himself so well all day that even a heavier dinner would not exceed the limits of his diet.

That kind of thing is easier for some people than others. Claudia Wilbourn, for example, is another who finds it easier to maintain a diet than many bodybuilders she knows.

"Basically," she explains, "I'm not food oriented. Since I don't get that much pleasure from eating, I can just pick at a meal and end up eating very little. But I've seen other people, even bodybuilders getting ready for contests, who had to be practically handcuffed to keep them from reaching for more food."

Just as in training, there are individual differences in eating behavior among bodybuilders. There are some bodybuilders who have to drag themselves into the gym every day, and others who almost have to be dragged away. The same thing can occur at the dinner table. If you happen to be someone for whom discipline comes easily, enjoy it. If not, you're just going to have to work at it.

When you aren't trying to get into contest shape, all you really have to do is exercise a little judgment and restraint. This means simply:

1. Don't eat too much.
2. Don't eat junk.

"Junk" is a relative term when applied to food. Take pizza, for example. If you aren't trying to get into contest shape, a slice of pizza won't hurt you. It's high in starch and other carbohydrates, and the cheese contains a lot of fat. But a small portion won't make you fat as long as you don't go over your caloric limit for the day.

If, on the other hand, you're a marathon runner, you might want to polish off a whole pizza and then order a plate of spaghetti, because that kind of endurance activity requires an enormous amount of carbohydrate energy.

Junk food is also anything that's so highly processed that its nutritional value is destroyed—or it can be so high in sugar, fat, chemicals and additives that it's simply no longer qualified to be called a food.

But competition bodybuilders have to be much more disciplined about food than most other athletes. They need to lose almost as much body fat as the marathon runner, but they can't burn it off through exercise. Their body fat has to be controlled largely by diet, and that means getting all their nutritional needs while eating as few calories as necessary. So pizza and spaghetti just don't qualify.

"I try to arrive at where the contest is being held just the night before the event," says Bill Grant, "and that minimizes the problem. But when I do go to restaurants, I end up eating an awful lot of omelettes."

Eggs *do* make a good meal for a bodybuilder on the road, but there are a few problems with this particular food. For one thing, eggs contain about as much fat as they do protein—six grams—so you don't want to eat too many. Also, omelettes are fried, and frying adds more fat and thus more calories. Ideally, you should try to eat some of your eggs boiled or poached to avoid this.

"Airline food is the worst for a bodybuilder," Bill Grant told me, "so I try to bring along my own food. I usually have some hard-boiled eggs and some tuna so I don't have to eat all that airline starch."

Bodybuilders on the road get quite familiar with tuna, tuna salad, salads in general and hamburger patties. Some order cottage cheese,

Bill Grant's secrets to looking this cut up in a contest are arriving the night before the event and eating omelettes when he goes out to restaurants.

but Mandy Tanny believes this is not a good idea.

"Cheese contains a lot of fat," she says. "And processed cheese, like most processed foods, has a lot of salt and chemicals added. I would recommend, instead, going with fish, chicken and fresh vegetables and fruit, just as you would at home."

Mandy points out that frequently it's the better restaurants that give you the widest choice. For example, if you order fish in a fast-food joint, it almost always comes breaded and deep-fried. In a good restaurant, however, you can get your fish broiled and you can substitute some other vegetable for french fries.

Even eating salads can present hazards to bodybuilders trying to stay cut up. For one thing, most dressings are high in calories—about 100 in a tablespoon. So never order a salad unless you

specify that the dressing should be on the side, and then put on just enough for taste. If you're dipping into a salad bar, remember that all those ingredients are not equal. Potato or macaroni salad is usually full of mayonnaise. On the other hand, lettuce, celery, tomatoes, bean sprouts and the like are very low in calories and high in fiber.

Low-cal diet plates can be all right, but beware of "pressed" turkey and other processed foods. They may appear to be normal and nutritious, but you will find they've been altered quite a bit. Actually, that goes for eggs, too. If you find a restaurant that serves only scrambled eggs, it's probably because those eggs come out of a carton, not a shell, and have been highly processed.

Many bodybuilders are coffee drinkers, and they're finding that it's increasingly hard to get cream or milk for their coffee, even in good restaurants. Instead, some form of "non-dairy" chemical is offered. If you ask, however, most restaurants have some half-and-half or milk stashed away for those customers who prefer coffee without chemicals.

To sum up, here's a good set of rules for eating in restaurants while you're traveling:

1. Don't overeat—the best eating plan in the world won't keep you cut up if you eat too much.
2. Choose your restaurants carefully. Often, the better the restaurant, the more choice you'll have and the better the food will be prepared.
3. Avoid airline food. Eat before you get on the plane, or bring along a snack. However, you can usually get fruit, fruit juice and salads on aircraft, and sometimes the airline will provide acceptable dishes like tuna salad.
4. Remember, when you eat fried or scrambled eggs or an omelette, you're looking at extra calories added in the cooking.
5. Always ask how items on the menu are prepared. Is the fish broiled, baked or fried? Is it breaded? Be sure of what you are going to eat.
6. Always ask that sauces, dressings and toppings be given to you on the side. If you order toast, butter it yourself. Control what goes on your food.
7. Be sparing of salad dressings. Try a little lemon juice for low-cal taste.
8. If you need bread with a meal, specify what kind (whole wheat is nutritious and high in fiber). If you don't intend to eat the rolls or breadsticks, ask that they be removed.
9. If you sit down hungry, get a salad right away. Don't sit there until you get so hungry that you start eating the bread or overeat at dinner.
10. Substitute when you can. Get a fresh vegetable instead of french fries. Discuss it with your waitress. She'll probably be so impressed with your muscles that she'll make special arrangements.
11. Apply your nutritional knowledge. Baked potatoes, for example, are a really good diet food, if they aren't covered in sour cream or butter. If you keep to a balanced diet, with some protein, carbs and fat in your meals, you'll have more energy for the contest and look better onstage. If you go to extremes in denying yourself food, you'll throw your metabolism off and you won't look as good.

Of course, all your eating doesn't have to be in restaurants. As soon as you get to your hotel, find out the location of the nearest market or deli. There's nothing to keep you from stocking your own supply of eggs, lean meat, chicken, fruit and fruit juice. Nibbling a little at a time over a period of hours may result in a lower food intake than eating regular meals in the social setting of a restaurant.

A bodybuilder spends months getting ready for a contest and then, the day before, does something drastic and extreme to get an edge— and blows it. Or, after weeks of strenuous discipline and careful eating, a competitor thinks he or she is not cut up enough, and tries to get rid of the excess fat by fasting for two days before the event.

But that doesn't work. If you don't have your cuts by then, it's too late. Better to eat well the last few days and keep your energy level up. Posing is hard work, and you don't want to go onstage drained and fatigued. As I've said before, Arnold and Franco both tried to be five pounds too light a week before a contest so they could relax those last few days and eat what they wanted. An excellent practice.

If you've found a way of eating that helps you get into shape, stay with it, even on the road. Sure, you can't eat all the same things you do at home, but you can get pretty close.

Just stick to the rules, don't eat too much, don't eat junk, and use your head. If it seems tough, okay. Remember, if it were all that easy, then everyone would do it.

TRAINING PROGRAMS

Lou Ferrigno's Incredible Hulking Mass and Power Course

*by Lou Ferrigno
with Bill Reynolds*

Gaining muscular body weight and strength is a difficult task. If it wasn't, everyone would look like The Incredible Hulk and be able to lift like Vasili Alekseev.

It is, however, possible to gain both muscle mass and strength at an acceptable rate of speed if you go about it correctly. I started training at 14, when I was 5'9" and weighed barely 120 pounds soaking wet. And my skinny body was so weak that I couldn't bench press more than 65 pounds, regardless of how much I puffed and strained.

Now, almost 15 years later, I weigh 160 pounds more and I'm in top muscular condition. And even though I've never specialized in pure strength training, I can bench 420 pounds for reps. With specialized work, I'm sure I could easily bench 500 pounds.

Gaining both muscular mass and strength requires a combination of four factors:

1. Proper training
2. Good diet
3. Sufficient rest and sleep
4. Correct mental attitude

By following my suggestions in these four areas, you'll be able to gain both strength and muscular body weight.

TRAINING

At the most basic level, it's necessary to gain strength to gain weight. There's a direct correlation between the amount of weight you use in your exercises and the size of your muscles. The more you lift in the Bench Press and Squat, the larger your muscles will become.

Don't get confused, however, because muscle size doesn't automatically guarantee strength. Some 150-pound guys with 15-inch arms are so strong they can bench press 350 pounds. On the other hand, there are massive bodybuilders with 20-inch arms who can't bench 320.

While using heavier weights for reps in your workouts assures you of added muscle size, it takes low reps with extremely heavy weights to build the ligament and tendon power that assures you of great strength. Thus, small men with great muscle attachment strength are able to easily outlift bigger men who haven't trained specifically for muscle power.

Weight-gaining workouts have to be tailored to your metabolism. Slow gainers—who usually have very active metabolisms—generally have to do a lot less training than fast gainers. Slow gainers tend to run their energy reserves too low on longer workouts. Then they can't recuperate enough between workouts to grow, and often

63

Here they are—all of Incredible Lou's weight-gaining and power secrets.

they overtrain and actually begin to lose muscle size.

Recuperation plays a vital role in how fast you gain, and it's essential that your workouts are tailored to fit your recuperative abilities. I could write an entire article on the relationship between recuperation and weight gain, but Joe Weider penned an excellent series on recuperation in past issues of *Muscle & Fitness*. I suggest you read these articles thoroughly, plus pay close attention to the suggestions on sleep and rest I offer later in this article.

As you can see from what I've written so far, you'll need heavy, short workouts to gain weight—heavy to stimulate growth, short to allow recuperation and growth. The easiest way to do short workouts is to restrict them to basic exercises that work two or more large muscle groups at the same time. Flyes are much less effective as a chest exercise for muscle growth and strength increase than Bench Presses, for example. Flyes isolate resistance only in the pecs, while Benches work the pecs, delts and triceps (plus the lats, to some extent) simultaneously.

To train heavy and short on basic exercises, I would recommend that you pyramid your poundages. This involves using heavier weights

and lower reps on each succeeding set (e.g. Bench Press: 135 × 12; 205 × 10; 255 × 8; 305 × 6; 340 × 4; 360 × 2). This allows you to warm up thoroughly and still use the heaviest possible weights on each movement.

Combining all the above principles, here is a good weight-gain routine for hard gainers (do this workout on Mondays, Wednesdays and Fridays):

Exercise	Sets	Reps
1. Sit-Ups	1	25–40
2. Squats	5	12/10/8/6/4*
3. Deadlift	1	6–8
4. Barbell Bent Row	5	12/10/8/6/4*
5. Shrug	1	10–15
6. Bench Press	5	12/10/8/6/4*
7. Military Press	1	6–8
8. Barbell Curl	1	6–8
9. Calf Machine	3	15/12/10*

Indicates exercise in which you should pyramid your poundages.

You should be able to do this routine in one hour or less. If it takes longer, you're undoubtedly resting more than 60–75 seconds

between sets, which can allow your body to cool off and leave you open to injuries.

If you're a beginner (in other words, if you've trained less than six months), the above would be an appropriate routine for you. If you have trained less than six weeks, however, do only the first three sets of each exercise marked for pyramiding.

If you are more advanced—and are an easy gainer—try this four-day split routine (*never* train more than four days per week on a weight-gain routine, however):

Monday–Thursday

Exercise	Sets	Reps
1. Sit-Ups	1	25–50
2. Squats	5	12/10/8/6/4*
3. Leg Extensions	3	8–10
4. Deadlifts	3	10/8/6*
5. Barbell Bent Row	5	12/10/8/6/4*
6. Lat Pulldowns	5	12/10/8/6/4*
7. Shrugs	3	10–15
8. Barbell Curl	4	10/8/6/6*
9. Dumbbell Curl	4	19/8/6/6*
10. Wrist Curl	4	10–15
11. Standing Calf Machine	5	10–15

Tuesday–Friday

Exercise	Sets	Reps
1. Leg Raise	1	25–50
2. Bench Press	5	12/10/8/6/4*
3. Incline Press	5	12/10/8/6/4*
4. Military Press	4	12/10/8/6*
5. Upright Row	4	12/10/8/6*
6. Lying Triceps Extension	4	6–8
7. Lat Pushdown	4	6–8
8. Seated Calf Machine	5	10–15

Pyramid these exercises.

The above routine is good for developing strength, but for maximum power you'll need to do fewer reps. Try doing pyramids of 5–4–3–2–1 reps on the basic exercises. And once every two weeks you can do a Rest Pause routine of five sets of single reps on each of the exercises marked for pyramiding.

You should also specialize on power-rack exercises to improve the weak parts of specific lifts. If you have trouble with the middle range of a Bench Press, for example, set the pins on the rack so you can press a very heavy weight only over those difficult few inches. This will quickly strengthen your muscle attachments, which eliminates the weak link. Simply improving your power over the weak part of a lift will often drastically increase the amount of weight you can use for the whole movement.

DIET

The secret to a weight-gain diet is to eat small quantities of food 4–6 times per day, rather than the common 2–3 large meals each day. Protein builds muscle tissue, but your body can only digest and use 30–40 grams of protein per feeding. Because of this, it definitely makes sense to eat smaller meals more frequently.

I'd recommend that you eat 1–1½ grams of protein per pound of body weight. The best protein comes from animal sources, such as beef, fish, fowl, eggs and milk products. Beans, peas and grains are also good protein sources. But vegetable proteins lack one or two of the essential amino acids, so you'll have to combine these foods with other vegetable or animal protein sources to complete the amino acid balance.

You should eat a balanced diet to go with your protein. Concentrate on fresh fruits, fresh vegetables, green salads, nuts, seeds, grains and potatoes. I also suggest that each day you take one or two Mega-Paks of Weider "Good Life" vitamins and minerals as insurance against progress-halting nutritional deficiencies.

If you're worried about what to eat specifically, here's a suggested nutritional schedule for one day:

Meal 1 (8 a.m.)—Cheese omelette with 4–5 eggs, whole grain toast, piece of fruit, 1–2 glasses of raw milk.

Meal 2 (11 a.m.)—Two meat or cheese sandwiches on whole grain bread, 3 oz. of raw nuts, 1–2 glasses of raw milk.

Meal 3 (2 p.m.)—Tuna salad, piece of fruit sliced on yogurt, 1–2 glasses of raw milk.

Meal 4 (5 p.m.)—Protein drink (pint of raw milk, ⅓ cup of Weider Olympian 90% milk and egg protein powder, and fruit or another flavoring to taste). This should be your pre-workout meal, since it will give you an abundance of protein and training energy.

Meal 5 (8 p.m.)—Steak, vegetable, baked potato, 1–2 glasses of raw milk.

Meal 6 (11 p.m.)—3 oz. hard cheese, 3 oz. of raw sunflower seeds, 1–2 glasses of raw milk. Or, as an alternative to this, you can take another protein drink.

The pre-bedtime meal is essential since the calories and protein in this last meal aren't needed for normal daily activity and tissue repair. As a result, the nutrients in that meal are more readily available to build tissue while you sleep. You actually build the most muscle while sleeping!

Milk has long been touted as a weight-gain food, and raw milk is much superior to pasteurized milk for this purpose. However, some bodybuilders are allergic to the lactose (sugar) in milk. Since hard cheeses don't have lactose, you can simply increase your cheese intake to get the same effect as drinking 2–3 quarts of milk per day.

"Military Presses (above) are my favorite movement for shoulder mass and power. Be sure not to bend your torso backward as you press."

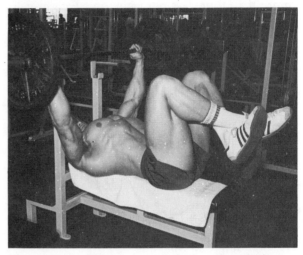

"Bench Presses (above) are one of the best upper body movements for strength and muscle mass. They primarily affect the pecs."

"Wrist Curls add club-like mass to my forearms and improve my grip strength. Note the narrow, thumbless grip."

"This Cable Lateral movement (right) isolates the rear deltoid. I'm showing it to you just so you'll know the type of movement to avoid when training for mass and power."

"Leverage Bar Rows are a good alternative exercise to Barbell Bent Rows. Rowing gives your back both width and thickness."

"Squats are the best single thigh and general lower body exercise you can do. I always do Squats in my routine."

"I always do ab work—Crunches in this photograph—when building mass, because you have to keep the waist down while adding body weight."

"Barbell Bent Rows combined with Squats and Bench Presses would give you a great full-body workout for size and power."

"I do Toe Raises on a standing calf machine for calf size and strength."

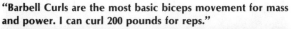

"Barbell Curls are the most basic biceps movement for mass and power. I can curl 200 pounds for reps."

"Seated, Standing, and Lying Triceps Extensions are all effective for bulking up and striating my triceps."

SLEEP AND REST

I mentioned the importance of recuperation as a prerequisite to muscle growth. The primary way your body recuperates is through sleep and rest. If you compared your recuperative balance to your checking account, workouts would be checks drawn (withdrawals), and sleep and rest would be deposits. Of course, you must have enough deposits to cover your checks or you'll go broke (overtrain).

The amount of sleep needed varies widely from individual to individual. It usually falls in the range of 8–10 hours per day. I'd recommend that you get as much sleep as possible. You can even take a half-hour nap in the afternoon, if that doesn't keep you awake at night.

Besides sleep, rest is also essential, particularly if you're a hard gainer. Limit your physical activities strictly to bodybuilding until you reach your muscle mass goals. A lot of champion bodybuilders run before contests, but you should never do that until you are in a cutting-up phase. If you want to look like a bodybuilder, bodybuild; if you want to look like a runner, run.

As a final component of the recuperation cycle, always try to keep your mind tranquil. If you're constantly nervous and worried about something, your body is burning up tremendous

amounts of nervous energy. Such energy should be directed into training and recuperation. So try to plug the energy leaks by staying calm and tranquil.

MENTAL ATTITUDE

Nothing is possible unless you truly *believe* it's possible. The mind is that powerful, and most top bodybuilders call the mind their strongest muscle.

In essence, your mental attitude must be totally positive. You must believe you can succeed, because you definitely can with the training, diet and recuperative procedures outlined in this article.

I suggest that you also practice the technique of *visualization*. Each night before you fall asleep, vividly imagine yourself the way you one day want to be. This triggers a psychological mechanism called the "self-fulfilling prophecy," which allows your mind to program you to achieve the image you've visualized. And that's not bad for 10–15 minutes of concentrated daydreaming before you fall asleep!

DRUGS

As you know from my past articles and columns, I've taken a positive stand on the limited use of anabolic steroids by competing bodybuilders. The weight-gain cycle is not an appropriate time to use steroids, however. They're best taken for 4–6 weeks before competing to hold muscle size as you diet.

Granted, you will gain weight on steroids, but you won't be able to hold the gains once you finally go off the drugs. That leads a lot of young bodybuilders to stay on steroids for long periods of time, and that's when you run the risk of encountering undesirable side effects. You'll be better off in the long run if you gain weight naturally, instead of with steroids. That's the way I gained.

FAT GAIN

When I was 19 I went from 220 pounds up to 315—a full 95 pounds—in seven months of heavy training and all-day eating. This may seem like a great gain, but a lot of fat came with the muscle. At 315 I had several spare tires around my waist. And when I got back into contest shape six months later—after a great struggle, I might add—I weighed only 221. That's an effective gain of only one pound in more than a year!

Believe me, bulking up and training down is not an effective way to gain muscle mass. Over the years I've discovered that I can't go more than 8–10 pounds over my contest weight and still retain maximum muscle mass once I train down. I've concluded, therefore, that bulking up and training down is a total and foolish waste of time for most bodybuilders.

As you gain weight, keep an eye on your abdominals. As soon as they blur out— particularly the intercostals and lower abdominals—you'll know you're getting too fat. Reduce your caloric intake and harden back up. It's best in the long run to gain weight slowly and patiently so that it's all muscle, rather than to merely pork up like I did 10 years ago.

CONCLUSION

In the final analysis, you're the one who will benefit from using this program regularly and to the best of your ability. Push hard in your training, add to your poundages whenever you can, never miss a workout, eat correctly, think positively, and sleep and rest enough for full recuperation. If you do, you'll be a lot bigger this time next year.

"Danny Padilla may be the Giant Killer, but this is one giant he's not after. We're great friends."

Chest Development

by Arnold Schwarzenegger

The chest is a very important body part to anyone entering bodybuilding competition. It must look good from every angle—standing relaxed in a line-up, in a side chest pose, in a Most Muscular shot, even in a double biceps pose.

Many good bodybuilders totally forget the pectorals in a double biceps shot, for example, but there should be a pectoral line when doing that pose. If your pecs disappear when your arms are up, you either don't have enough muscle there or you can't control it. The chest has to look good from all angles, or you'll never win Mr. Olympia.

Along with my biceps, the chest was quite good early on in my bodybuilding. It wasn't as easy as the biceps—indeed, several other areas were easier—but I seemed to train my chest hard and correctly from the very beginning. My training partners and I were familiar with the chest, back and biceps, so those body parts forged ahead and the rest lagged behind.

My chest grew because I gave it the most attention. I put a lot of energy into my chest training, and placed it first in my workout. That's a clear indication that you can improve any body part by using the Weider Muscle Priority Principle, since my chest didn't grow easily.

I was able to analyze chest training early in my career accurately enough to hit on a routine that I used with little variation for more than 10 years. Only the availability of more sophisticated training equipment—specifically, chest crossover cables—resulted in any additions to my early routine.

It was obvious to me that every area of the pectorals needed to be trained if complete development was expected. I had to work the upper, middle, lower, outer and inner pecs, plus the rib cage. And since I was after size and muscle mass in the early days, I knew that the routine had to be basic and very heavy. My instinct and research told me all of this.

My primary inspiration at the time was a collection of Reg Park photos that I had clipped from the few copies of *Muscle Builder* (now *Muscle & Fitness*) that came my way. He had both a huge rib cage and enormous pectorals, and every time I saw his famous side chest shot I knew that I wanted to soon be as good in the same pose. I was also impressed by the side chest shot of Vic Seipke on the cover of another old mag, as well as those of Chuck Sipes and Bruce Randall, both former Mr. Universe winners.

My early routine in Germany and Austria consisted of Bench Presses, Incline Presses, Flyes, Dips and Pullovers, each for five sets of 6–10

"Franco says the Bench Press is the best single chest exercise, while Vince claims it's 90% front delt and therefore worthless for the chest. In my opinion neither is right or wrong."

reps. I did the Bench Presses for overall pectoral development and for powerlifting strength, using different grip widths from time to time in order to get at the inner and outer pectoral muscles.

Incline Presses were for the upper pectorals, Flyes for the outer pecs (as well as the inner pectorals as the movement was brought to completion), Dips for the lower and a little of the outer pectorals, and Pullovers for the rib cage and pec finishing. The Pullovers were done with a dumbbell while lying across a bench.

Often I would combine lats with chest and then I'd do a Bent-Arm Pullover lying along the bench and using very heavy weights. This is like a pullover machine, and I'd do it mainly with an EZ-curl bar. I'd have someone sitting on my legs to keep me from pulling *myself* over instead of the bar.

While my Bench Presses were most often done for five sets of 6–10 reps, this would change when I was working toward a powerlifting competition. Then I might do 8–12 sets of Bench Presses while working up to a very heavy weight. Sometimes this was followed by many sets down to an empty bar.

At my best, I've done a 500-pound Bench Press. For reps my best efforts have been 405×8, 315×25 and 225×60. Eventually my goals shifted entirely to bodybuilding, but the powerlifting

"Dips are the basic lower pectoral exercise. They also hit the outer pecs a little."

had given me the strength to use mass-building poundages in my everyday training. In general, the size of the muscles grows with the size of the weights you are using for repetitions, so being strong is an advantage.

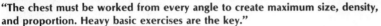

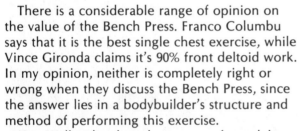

"The chest must be worked from every angle to create maximum size, density, and proportion. Heavy basic exercises are the key."

"Flyes are for the middle and outer pectorals."

There is a considerable range of opinion on the value of the Bench Press. Franco Columbu says that it is the best single chest exercise, while Vince Gironda claims it's 90% front deltoid work. In my opinion, neither is completely right or wrong when they discuss the Bench Press, since the answer lies in a bodybuilder's structure and method of performing this exercise.

Ken Waller developed enormous front delts from doing Bench Presses, while his pecs benefited little. He had to do a lot of Flyes and Crossovers to get his pecs up, because his structure prevented him from getting full value from Benches. He also tended to press the barbell up with his elbows in close to his sides, which further complicated the matter.

Franco, on the other hand, could isolate the pectoral muscles very well with Bench Presses by the way he held his chest and kept his elbows straight under the bar as he pressed it up. He also had the right bone structure for most of the Bench Press to hit his pecs. It was the same with Mike Katz, who was always noted for his phenomenal chest. Despite having long arms, he always pulled back his elbows to isolate his pecs.

So you can see that both Vince and Franco are right and wrong at the same time. The truth depends on structure and bench-press style. If you want to do the Bench Press, you should be sure to keep the elbows straight out to the sides

as you press. You should also endeavor to keep your chest high.

It's essential to find out, using the Weider Instinctive Training Principle, what are the best exercises for your body. You may be the type of person—like Serge Nubret, who does 20 sets of 15–20 reps on the Bench Press and little else for his chest—who was born to do Benches. In Nubret's case, Vince Gironda's view is totally wrong. Or you may need Flyes and Crossovers almost exclusively, like Waller, which would make Franco wrong. With every single muscle group, we have to find which exercises—and ways of doing exercises—are best for our individual bodies.

There seems to be controversy over whether or not Pullovers will expand the rib cage, some saying that they will, others that they won't. I've always done Pullovers in my own routine, and gained several inches in my rib cage from them, so I'm sure you know which side has my sentiment and support. Pullovers expanded and lifted my rib cage considerably, and also helped me learn how to hold a rib cage pose.

Essentially, Pullovers stretch the cartilages that attach your ribs to your sternum, the bone

START/"Cable Crossovers gave me great pectoral cuts."/FINISH

START/"Pullovers expand the rib cage and finish off the pectorals."/FINISH

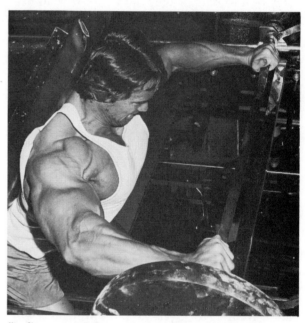

"Inclines were always my basic upper chest exercise."

running down the middle at the front of your chest. By gradually stretching this connective tissue, your rib cage will grow larger in volume.

Some experts say that it's virtually impossible to stretch the rib cage past the age of about 18–19, when the body has almost completely stopped growing. In my opinion, you don't necessarily have to be at a young age, although it's easier to change anything in your body when younger. I've seen people improve the rib cage in their 30s and 40s.

A large rib cage is essential to a perfect body, because it contributes to the whole. You need to have a good side chest pose and can't do one

without a large rib cage. The rib cage also lends size to the entire upper body, since it lays a large foundation for shoulder width, back depth and chest.

I was aware early, however, that a large rib cage can also make the shoulders visually narrower, because people like George Eifferman tended to look narrower in the shoulders. On the other hand, a guy like Steve Reeves—with his shallower chest—appeared much wider in the shoulders. Still, this is a small disadvantage when offset by the side chest shot and other poses when a rib cage is full.

Let's move up to my chest training programs for the '75 Olympia. Keep in mind, however, that the programs were constantly changing within a basic framework. I liked to shock the muscles by not letting them get complacent and relaxed in a consistent routine. If they didn't know what to expect each workout, they had to grow more.

Prior to the '75 Olympia I did my chest with lats as the morning half of my Weider Double Split on Mondays, Wednesdays and Fridays. By then I was doing Inclines before Benches, since I felt I needed to put more priority on the upper chest. I did routines like this:

1. Incline Press: 5 × 8–10
2. Bench Press: 5 × 8–10
3. Flyes: 5 × 8–10
4. Cable Crossovers: 5 × 10–15

I did not do dips anymore because I felt my pectorals were low enough. Cable Crossovers were for the cuts. I would also go up in weight on each set of the basic exercises, while gradually reducing the repetitions. The Inclines, for example, started out at 20 reps and then reduced down to 15–12–10–8, the weight increasing to 315 pounds. Some days, however, the reps would stay higher or go lower for more

of a shocking effect.

As you will recall from the biceps article I mentioned earlier, posing after my training for a body part was vital. I would spend quite a bit of time flexing my fully pumped chest at a variety of angles. This gave me muscle control, the ability to bring out more striations and enough endurance to pose for an entire Mr. Olympia prejudging.

In general, my exercise form was fairly strict, with only a cheating rep or two to force out extra movements at the end of a heavy set. The trick to bodybuilding is to put an overload on the muscles. The secret isn't so much to just get the weight up as it is to push up a heavy weight with the isolated strength of the muscles you're trying to train. Thus, strict form becomes essential.

The most common mistake in chest training is lack of concentration. It's so important to flex the pectoral muscles throughout the movement, but especially at the top. A second mistake is to follow someone else's routine set for set, having no concern about what's good for your own individual body. And a third is failing to stretch your pectorals enough. I used to do my Inclines a lot with dumbbells in order to get a better stretch in the upper pecs. The dumbbells can be lowered deeper than a barbell, which comes down against your chest before you can reach full stretch.

In conclusion, I feel that anything and everything is possible when it comes to developing the chest. I don't think I had particularly good heredity for chest development, and yet my chest came up quite well by using all the techniques I've mentioned in this article. If you follow these suggestions faithfully, I may one day see you on stage at the Universe. I may even see you picking up the winner's trophy!

Look at My Back Now!

by Chris Dickerson

Although I had certain natural talents for bodybuilding, the ability to develop an Olympian back was not among them. At a time when I was winning the Mr. USA, Mr. America and other national AAU titles, my back was underdeveloped. But look at it now! Today I'm not afraid to do back shots next to anyone!

I have always trained my back hard, but it steadfastly refused to make any real progress until about five years ago. My deltoids became large, round, well-balanced and deeply scored with striations, while my back remained flat and relatively narrow.

Those deltoids of mine were both a blessing and a curse. Because they were so good, they took the attention of the contest judges away from my back when I did my double-biceps shot and my twisting back poses.

But the deltoids also distracted my own mind focus from my back. I'd do Lat Pulldowns and I'd feel them in all three delt heads, but not in my lats. I'd feel Bent Rows in my posterior delts. I'd even feel Shrugs in my deltoids more than in my traps.

The turning point for me came five years ago when I saw a photo of my back in *Muscle Builder* (now *Muscle & Fitness*). It had been taken when I won the Mr. USA title seven or eight years before. When the photo first appeared, I had thought my double-biceps shot looked great, but I'd grown older and more objective over the years. When I looked at the shot again, I was mortified at how weak my back looked.

Weak muscle groups distress me because I'm totally devoted to building a perfectly proportioned physique. I immediately decided to specialize both mentally and physically on my back. As a result of this specialization, it began to look a great deal better within a few months.

Today I take great satisfaction in a photo I have taped to my bathroom mirror. I look at that picture every time I shave or brush my teeth. It's an exceptionally clear shot that Bill Reynolds took of my back at the '79 Canada Cup competition.

When I look at that photo, I am reassured that my back has—after years of toil on my part—finally reached superstar status. My back now has good thickness, flaring lats, proportionately balanced traps, lats and erectors, and excellent muscularity, even in total repose. Damn, I'm proud of that photo!

So how did I bomb my back hard enough to improve it from zero to 10? The first step was to gear up mentally for the task. I deliberately

began to think more about my back. I put the Weider Priority Principle into action, exercising my back first in the workout. I started doing my back training without a shirt on, just so I could see it in the mirror as I worked out. And I purposefully and systematically tried to feel every rep of every exercise solely in my back muscles.

With my mind in gear, I structured a routine that would develop all three areas of my back, but which would improve my lats faster than my traps and erectors. Formerly, competitors in the Mr. America received extra points for weightlifting ability. For that reason, I had put in some practice in Olympic-style weightlifting. As a result, my traps and erectors became considerably more developed than my lats.

Contrary to my situation, however, you might lack trap development. So, let's discuss how to develop that muscle group. Power Cleans are one of the best back movements you can do, but this exercise is very difficult to learn. It's much easier to do Upright Rows and one or another version of the Shoulder Shrug.

Be sure your elbows are up and shoulders back at the top of your Upright Rows, and use a relatively narrow grip. I personally prefer doing Shrugs with a couple of dumbbells because I get a longer and freer movement. But you can use a barbell, or you can do Shrugs on the Bench-Press station of a Universal Gym. There's even a Nautilus machine designed exclusively for Shrugs.

Beginners can get a very good trapezius workout by doing just three sets (8–12 reps per set) of Upright Rows. Intermediates should add three sets of Shrugs to the beginners' routine. Aim for slightly higher reps (12–15 is about right) and use heavier weights.

Advanced bodybuilders should adjust their workouts for their trapezius (and, indeed, for every muscle group) according to how well or how poorly that body part is developing. You could do as many as 10–12 sets of Upright Rows and a variation or two of Shrugs if your traps are weak. Since mine were relatively strong, my trap workout consisted of only these exercises, sets and reps:

1. Upright Rows: 3 × 8–12 (three sets, 8–12 reps)
2. Dumbbell Shrugs: 2 × 12–15
3. Barbell Shrugs (in power rack): 2 × 10–12

There are a number of very effective exercises for the powerful erector spinae muscles running up each side of your spinal column from your buttocks to the lower insertion of the traps. Both of the Olympic lifts (the Snatch and the Clean and Jerk), as well as the Deadlift, are excellent for developing the erector spinae. That's why weightlifters and powerlifters have such thick backs.

START/Lat Pulldown/FINISH

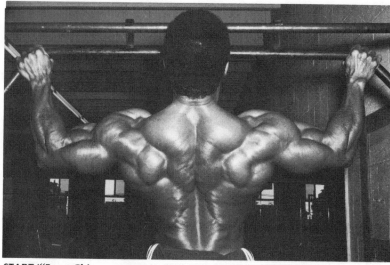

START/"Front Chins are great for lat width! From a full stretch, pull up as high as you can, being sure to arch your back throughout the movement."/FINISH

START/"Barbell Bent Rows (below) are an excellent movement for increasing your back thickness. Note how my back muscles bunch up at the finish."/FINISH

START/"For building both thickness and width in your back, nothing can equal Seated Pulley Rows (below)."/FINISH

START/"T-Bar Rows are another excellent movement for building width. Notice how I can improve the range of movement by standing on a block."/FINISH

START/"The best single back-thickness exercise for me has always been Dumbbell Bent Rowing. I prefer to kneel on the bench, but this exercise can also be done standing."/FINISH

Bodybuilders often do Deadlifts, but with higher reps and more moderate poundages than a powerlifter would use. Our objective is not to see how much we can lift but to build muscle tissue. Heavy single reps can easily injure your back, so I'd recommend that you avoid extremely heavy Deadlifts.

The lower back exercises most commonly used by bodybuilders are the Good Morning, the Hyperextension and the Stiff-Leg Deadlift. All three movements are excellent for your lower back *if* you use light weights and your reps are in the 8–15 range.

I like to see beginners start off by doing three sets (10–15 reps per set) of Hyperextensions with no added weight. Hyperextensions stretch your spine, while Good Mornings and all types of Deadlifts have a slight compression effect on your vertebrae and the discs between them. If you have any sort of lower back pain, the only erector spinae movement you should do is Hyperextensions.

Intermediates can do their three sets of Hyperextensions with barbell plates held behind their heads for added resistance. I'd also suggest doing 2–3 sets of Stiff-Leg Deadlifts, with your reps in the 8–12 range. As a bonus, these Deadlifts will also improve your hamstrings.

Again, advanced bodybuilders should adopt a training routine appropriate to the quality of their erector spinae development. At most, you should do 3–4 sets each of Hyperextensions, Stiff-Leg Deadlifts and Good Mornings 2–3 times a week.

To develop my weak lats, I knew I had to do exercises for both width and thickness. Width-building movements include all the various forms of Chins and Pulldowns, while all variations of Barbell and Dumbbell Bent Rows build thickness. Pulley Rows are unique in that they build both thickness and width.

Beginners should stick to a lat routine consisting of one exercise for width development (Lat Pulldowns to the front of the neck) and one for thickness (Barbell Bent Rows). Do 2–3 sets of each exercise, 8–10 reps per set.

As you gradually gain strength and endurance, increase the number of sets.

Intermediates can do a total of about five sets for width and five sets for thickness. Here's a good routine along these lines (it includes Barbell Pulley Rows, which—as we said—is a lat width *and* thickness movement):

1. Dumbbell Bent Rows: 4 × 8–10
2. Chins Behind the Neck: 4 × 8–10
3. Seated Pulley Rows: 3 × 8–10

Advanced bodybuilders will benefit from using part—or all—of my lat specialization routine. If your lats are good, do two sets of each movement. If they're only fair, do three sets of each exercise. And if they're very poor, do four sets of each movement, as I did.

Here's the lat specialization routine I used:

1. Chins (to the front of my neck): 4–5 × 10–15 (with weight added on the final 2–3 sets)
2. Dumbbell Bent Rows: 4–6 × 8–10
3. Pulldowns Behind the Neck: 4 × 8–10
4. One-Arm Pulley Rows: 4 × 8–10
5. Seated Pulley Rows: 4 × 8–10

I worked hardest on Dumbbell Bent Rowing because I consider it to be one of the best—if not *the* best—lat exercises. I also put a lot of energy into the Seated Pulley Rows because they were last in my routine and I wanted to be sure to have thoroughly exhausted my lats by the time I finished the workout.

I did this back specialization workout, plus abs and a little calf work, on Mondays and Thursdays. I worked my chest, shoulders and biceps Tuesdays and Fridays, and my thighs, triceps and forearms Wednesdays and Saturdays. I think you have to devote almost a full workout to a body part on which you're specializing. That allows you to focus all of your mental and physical energies on that muscle group, and as a result it simply *has* to grow.

Good luck with my routine. I hope it works as well for you as it did for me!

Shoulders like a Greek God's:
Arnold's Deltoid Routine

by Arnold Schwarzenegger
as told to Bill Reynolds

"The importance of shoulders in the male physique goes all the way back to the ancient Greeks," says Arnold Schwarzenegger. "I remember once seeing a diagram illustrating the visual impact of the body. It was in the form of an X—starting with the shoulders, crossing at the abdominals and ending at the calves. These are the areas that give the most immediate impression of male strength."

One error young bodybuilders often make, Arnold believes, is they fail to realize that the shoulders are a complex body part. We tend to think in terms of having wide shoulders to promote a V-shaped torso, but an examination of the anatomy of the shoulders reveals there's a lot more to them than width.

"First of all you have the deltoids. These muscles serve to raise your arm above your head. But the joint where the arm meets the torso is a complex one. Unlike a joint such as the knee, which has a limited range of motion and moves basically in one plane, the shoulder joint lets you move your arm around in a circle and with a very wide range of motion.

"Muscles are simple. They contract in only one direction. So when you want movement in several directions, you need several different muscles. Or you need a complex muscle group. And that's exactly what the deltoids are."

Powerful shoulders are fundamental to a powerful physique.

80

In order to cope with the complex movement of the shoulder joint, Arnold points out, the deltoids consist of three basic heads. The technical names for these parts of the muscle group are the anterior, medial and posterior deltoid—or more commonly, the front, side and rear.

"There's no one exercise that will work all three areas of the deltoids," says Arnold. "Some work two, but not all three. Therefore, when you're planning your shoulder routine, you have to include the right variety of movements so that you get full shoulder development."

Arnold has always been in favor of using poses to check one's physical progress. After all, a bodybuilder onstage is most carefully scrutinized by the judges when he's actually hitting a pose. Exercise routines should be geared to developing your appearance when posing, not when you're just standing around. And when you hit a pose in front of the mirror, sometimes you discover new things about the body.

"Many people don't realize that shoulders are tremendously important in hitting back shots," Arnold explains. "Take the rear double-biceps pose, for example. What is it you show in that pose? Look carefully and you'll see that the deltoid development merges into the trapezius development. And the traps dominate the whole upper center of the back."

Arnold has found that a lot of young bodybuilders underestimate the traps. They think of this muscle group as contributing mostly to that line that extends down from the neck to the deltoids. In fact, these muscles extend down in a diamond shape, between the lats, well down toward the lower back.

"You need good lats and a good lower back," Arnold goes on, "but you won't be able to impress the judges with your back poses until you have also fully developed the deltoids and trapezius muscles. You've got to have it all. Having just part of it won't make the grade."

The shoulder girdle musculature also includes the pectoralis minor of the upper chest, but this area is normally developed through an adequate chest routine. So the main concern in working out a routine to produce championship-quality shoulders is to employ exercises that work all three deltoid heads, and fully hit the trapezius muscles.

"The two basic exercises for the deltoids are various kinds of Shoulder Presses, and a number of different Lateral Raises. The standard Military Press, in which a barbell is lifted from chest height straight overhead, obviously works the heads of the deltoids in a slightly different way than does a Press Behind the Neck. I like to do both, sometimes together in the same workout, sometimes in alternate workouts."

Arnold also employs Dumbbell Presses in his shoulder routine. To give him a different effect than he gets in the Barbell Press, he takes pains to lower the dumbbells several inches below the bottom position of the barbell movement, and to bring them together at the top. This promotes a greater range of motion.

"One mistake I see bodybuilders make frequently in doing a Press," says Arnold, "is they lock out on top. Once you lock your elbows, you have taken most of the stress off the muscles. If you stop just below locking out, you increase the effect of the exercise."

Arnold also uses another variation of the Dumbbell Press that he calls the "Arnold Press." In this movement, he begins by holding the dumbbells as he would at the top of a Dumbbell Curl. Then he presses them upward, rotating his thumbs inward. This gives him an exercise that's part press and part lateral, and which works both the anterior and medial deltoid heads.

"Laterals are great because, depending on what plane you confine the movement to, you can work any part of the deltoid you wish. Dumbbell Front Laterals work the front, Side Laterals the side, and Bent-Over Laterals the rear."

Arnold also does a movement called Lying Side Laterals, in which he lies on his side on an abdominal board and raises a dumbbell from this position. He may not have invented this exercise, but when he first came to California you suddenly saw a lot of people who'd never performed the movement before doing Lying Side Laterals. One bodybuilder theorized that Arnold likes to make up new movements just to show how other people in the gym are copying him. However, this is a movement that Arnold really believes in and practices.

"Cable exercises add even more variety to your shoulder workouts," he says. "One-Arm Side Cable Laterals give you a constant tension throughout the movement. You can have the cable cross in front of you or behind you, and each approach has a different feel. In fact, there are numerous kinds of shoulder lifts you can do to increase the effect of your shoulder workout."

For trap development, Arnold relies on four basic exercises—Power Pulls, Cleans, Upright Rows and Shoulder Shrugs.

"I always preferred to do my Barbell Presses seated, regardless of whether I pressed the bar from the front or the back of my neck."

"To hit the whole delt I did Rotating Dumbbell Presses. Note how my hands rotate 180 degrees as I press the dumbbells."

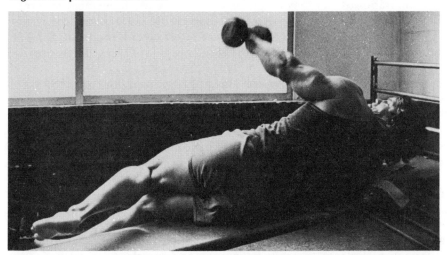

"The Alternate Front Raise (below) complements Presses for the anterior deltoid head. It's important to raise the dumbbells alternately to prevent any cheating with the weights."

"The Lying Side Lateral Raise (above) is an excellent movement for finishing off the rear and side delts, and the perfect movement for the posterior deltoid head has for me always been Cable Bent Laterals (below).

"Cleaning a weight involves a good, satisfying effort of coordination, but you shouldn't start out with too heavy a weight. For Power Pulls, you can go for more weight, because you're essentially doing Cleans but not letting the weight get above your chest or below your waist.

"When you do Upright Rows I think it's important to keep the movement smooth and slow. Don't go jerking the weight up or letting it drop. And with Shrugs, an awful lot of bodybuilders use too much weight so that they don't lift the shoulders as high as possible. It doesn't do much good to try to lift 100 pounds and only complete half the movement."

Using the Weider Split-Routine Principle, Arnold likes to train delts and arms together, working the delts first. Because the deltoid-trapezius complex is such a complicated muscle group structure, he does more sets than many other bodybuilders—as many as 50 sets in some cases, but at least 30–35 in a normal workout.

"I know there's a lot of talk about needing only five sets for a body part. Still, I just don't see how you can train your entire shoulder area with just five sets. If you consider that the deltoids are really three muscles and the traps are about as complex, you're really training six different body parts, and six multiplied by five equals 30 sets."

One form of exercise Arnold uses is among the simplest but most overlooked—posing.

"Posing is exercise. You're contracting the muscles to their maximum. I always flex and pose the muscles I'm exercising. I think that's had a lot to do with my success in bodybuilding."

But Arnold also realizes that the same kind of routine which is right for him might not be the best for everyone. A beginner, for example, should not try to equal the amount of energy Arnold puts into his training.

"I like to see a beginner take his time building up his strength and stamina. For example, one way to really get the delts to respond is to work with lighter weights and do more reps per set. Pump the blood through those muscles and get them to come alive. And don't try to do too many different kinds of exercises in one workout. Doing an Overhead Press, Standing Laterals, Bent-Over Laterals, Upright Rows and Shrugs is plenty. And when you're going for growth, don't hurry to get into supersetting. You grow more just doing straight sets."

Working to perfect your shoulder workouts, says Arnold, can make the difference between a so-so or a first-rate physique. "Look at how we think of shoulders," he point out. "You 'shoulder a burden.' Someone has 'the world on his shoulders.' You put your 'shoulder to the wheel.' This tradition has stayed alive since the ancient Greeks for a reason—powerful shoulders are fundamental to a powerful physique."

"Dumbbell Side Laterals should be done bent slightly forward with your arms rounded throughout the movement."

My Hulking 23+ Arm Workout

by Lou Ferrigno
with Bill Reynolds

Bodybuilding needs a new leader, and it's no secret that I hope to fill that role. Arnold was the leader for many years, but he hasn't been in shape since 1975. The sport needs to have a dominant bodybuilder leading the parade, and I want to be that man.

During the past couple of years I didn't have this desire. Now I do. When the Hulk series first came along, I was in incredible condition, literally ready to sweep away all opposition at the Olympia. But with the long and irregular hours I put in filming the weekly television series, I began to slip out of top shape. Faced with a 2:00 a.m. workout and a 6:00 a.m. call the next day, it was tough to go into the gym, let alone to train hard.

I slacked off on my training for the first 1½ years of the Hulk, but things are different now. Today's kids need a physical idol—a hero—and since I'm in the best position to provide this positive body image, the onus is on me to be in great shape. The thousands of fan letters I have received from kids around the world has rekindled my desire to become a legend. Once again, I want to be the greatest bodybuilder who ever lived, a goal I've had since my youth.

Bodybuilding is my first and greatest love in life, and it will remain with me forever. Still, I have to push myself hard mentally to train. It's never easy to train when you work as much as I do, but if you want it you'll train and train hard. I want it.

Some days I get only a couple hours of sleep, but two hours of sleep or 10, I'm in the gym six days per week. And it's amazing how much progress I've made lately. The improvement has been so quick and dramatic that all my friends at the World Gym—the only place I'll train—have been asking me if I'll give the Olympia a shot this year.

Right now I'm only two weeks from Olympia-winning condition. Two weeks of tight dieting would put me there. I also badly miss being on stage in competitive shape. Obviously, it's a tremendous temptation to go into the Olympia and scrap the plans of Zane, Robby, Mentzer, Coe, Callender, Padilla and all the rest.

So am I going? I can't say yes and I can't say no, because somebody will think I'm full of it either way. I'll just keep people guessing and keep training to get into better and better shape. Maybe I'll just find the three months of uninterrupted training I'd like to have if I decided to compete again.

All of this leads me to a discussion of arm training, because I've been getting amazing

results with my new workout. It's pushed my arms up to 23+ pumped (believe it or not, they were under 13 inches when I first started bodybuilding!). Undoubtedly, I can tell you something about arm development that will help you make gains in that area.

The general public is fascinated by big arms. Among the hundreds of fan letters I get each week, more than 25% seem to ask how I've build such big arms. This interest pleases my ego, but it would be a disaster if I let this go to my head to the point where I went overboard on building even larger arms.

While size, shape and definition are important, the most vital consideration for any competing bodybuilder is *proportion*. There must be a pleasing balance between each of the major body parts, and any over- or under-developed area will result in lost points at a bodybuilding show.

Besides proportion, there are four other vital qualities to a good arm: (1) Size (thickness, roundness); (2) Shape (height, peak); (3) Density/Cuts; and (4) Vascularity. My main objective is to get full development of both the biceps and triceps so that they look massive from all angles. This full look has been characteristic of all those bodybuilders over the years—from Larry Scott to Arnold Schwarzenegger—who have been noted for great arms.

Hereditary factors have a lot to do with the shape of a muscle mass. If you're lucky, you'll have peaks on both your biceps and triceps, and they'll be lined up so that a tape passed over both would run at a 90-degree angle to your *humeris* bone. I've been doubly lucky with my biceps, since I have both natural peak and fullness, sort of a combination between Scott and Arnold.

Vascularity is a quality that goes hand in hand with hard training and a tight diet. Vascularity results from the diet, while the actual vein size results from a long period of hard training. The harder you train, the bigger the veins get, especially if you do a lot of supersets and trisets.

I feel that 12–15 sets are plenty for biceps and triceps, even for top bodybuilders. Some guys do 20–30 sets for biceps and the same for triceps every workout. This either overtrains them or results in less intense workouts. When you have to pace yourself over 30 sets, you're bound to be holding something back during the first few sets. I'd rather go hard all the way.

It would be a mistake for beginners and intermediates to try doing 15 sets. After a lot of experimenting with friends, I feel that beginning bodybuilders will grow best on 4–6 sets and intermediates on 8–10 sets of arm work.

On all of my arm exercises I like to do five sets, starting at 60% of my maximum and building up to 70, 80, 90 and 100% over the five sets. This guarantees that I'm fully warmed up when I'm on the heaviest sets, which, by the way, is why I've had so few training injuries.

For years I trained biceps and triceps on the same day, although lately I've been doing them on separate days. I found that I was losing a little concentration when training them together, and I was also probably resting too much.

These days I'm training chest and triceps on Mondays and Thursdays, back and biceps on Tuesdays and Fridays, and shoulders and legs on Wednesdays and Saturdays. I feel it's important to do biceps on pulling days and triceps when you push, because the arms are warmed up after doing the torso movements that involve the arms. I simply like to have my arms warmed up before I do any direct work on them.

I don't go quite as heavy as I used to in my workouts, because I'm using slightly higher reps now and concentrating more. The poundages are as heavy as I can handle for 8–10 reps with short rests between sets. I proved how strong I was in powerlifting and I feel I don't need to prove it again. Extremely heavy weight and low reps give me plenty of size, but not the separations and striations.

It's also important to use very strict form on all but the last couple of reps of each set, when you can loosen it up a little to force out a few more. I like to use forced reps on a couple of exercises per workout, but only on the last set, because I'll overtrain if I do too many forced-rep sets.

A final important factor in my arm training is the subtle changes I make in the exercises from one workout to the next. The exercises themselves are changed monthly, but the angles of each are varied from workout to workout. As an example, I might do Incline Curls on a 45-degree bench one day and at a 30-degree angle the next. Or I might curl the weights out a little more from my body than usual.

My biceps workout starts with Dumbbell Curls, which I do for shape and mass. I place a lot of my attention on fully supinating my hands as the weights come up. My first set is with 50-pound dumbbells, and over five sets of 8–10 reps I work up to a pair of 80s.

Next, I do five sets of 8–10 reps on the close-grip Preacher Curl. This is for the lower and

Slow, continuous-peak-contraction **Cable Curl.**

One-arm continuous tension **Dumbbell Curl.**

Dumbbell Curls.

START/**"Incline Curls are great for biceps fullness."**/FINISH

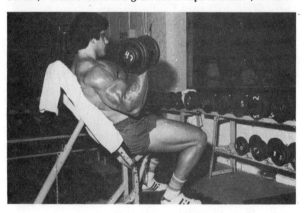

outer biceps, as well as for roundness in the belly of the muscle. I use an EZ-curl bar and curl it right up to my neck for a peak contraction.

My biceps are finished off with Incline Dumbbell Curls, in the usual 5 × 8–10 routine. Occasionally, I'll do a sixth set with 50% of my max, forcing out as many reps as I can for a burn-out. When I do Incline Curls, the dumbbells usually travel out at a 45-degree angle from my body.

Turning to triceps, I begin with 5 × 8–12 in the Lying Triceps Extension, working up to 175 pounds in good form. I lower the bar to a point behind my head, instead of to the forehead as so many bodybuilders do in this movement. It's sort of a combination of a pullover and an extension. Bringing the bar to my forehead doesn't give me enough stretch, and it's hard on my elbows. On all extensions, it's vital to keep your elbows in close to each other.

Lat Pushdowns are next on my list for triceps. Again, I do 5 × 8–12, working the poundage up. I've found it essential to stand upright and close to the pulley. I've also developed a preference for the short, angled handle over a straight and/or longer one. You can also use a rope handle on these if you like.

I finish off my triceps with 5 × 8–15 in the Seated Barbell Triceps Extension. At times I'll brace my back against a preacher bench on these, and I always keep my elbows pointed upward. Touching the bar at the base of my

neck seems to give me the best stretch. On all triceps exercises, I am sure to lock out at the completion, which causes that sharp horseshoe separation at the sides of your triceps.

In some modified form, this workout should add size, shape, density and vascularity to any bodybuilder's upper arms. Give it a try, but be sure to keep your arms in proportion to the rest of your body. Pump iron!

"The Lat Pushdown (left and above) affects the outer head of my triceps."

START/"The Preacher Curl hits my lower and outer biceps."/FINISH

START/"The Lying Triceps Extension bulks the long head of the triceps."/FINISH

START/"Cable Bent Laterals blast the rear deltoid and triceps."/FINISH

START/"Using an EZ-curl bar and keeping my elbows up are keys to directly hitting the triceps while doing the Seated Triceps Extension."/FINISH

Bigger Biceps:
Bodybuilding's Most Common Goal

by Boyer Coe

It is a cliche to say that the biceps are the showiest muscles on the male physique. But the fact that the observation is made by just about everybody who writes a book on exercise or who does an article on arm development doesn't make it any less true.

Everybody is fascinated with big arms, and to most people "big arms" mean big biceps. In fact, if you went out on the street and asked John Q. Public to show you his muscles, chances are that he would roll up his sleeve, flex his arm, and try to raise some kind of a lump there. Even in a physique contest, the first thing that most people are likely to notice is the comparative arm size of the participants. And each participant, undoubtedly, has worked backstage to get such a pump in the arms that some of these men look, at least momentarily, as though they have a pair of hams hanging from their shoulders.

Obviously, therefore, biceps are a high priority of bodybuilders everywhere, at all levels of development. Indeed, many of them first become interested in the sport because they want big arms. Go into any gym in the country and I'll wager that you will find more bodybuilders working on arms than any other single body part.

In the seminars I give around the country, the most commonly asked questions concern my arms and legs. But the fellows who want to know how to develop a split in the biceps somehow always seem to make themselves the first heard. So I usually start each session with a rundown of what I have done to build my biceps, how I trained for last year's Mr. Olympia, and what I am doing to build on my previous biceps development.

What many of these guys are looking for, of course, is a "secret" to getting big biceps—the kind that helped Arnold, in no small part, win his Mr. Olympia title seven times, the kind with which Sergio used to amaze his audience, the impossibly high-peaked kind that Robby has, or even the kind I have, which came from working them very hard for size, shape and peak almost from the time I first became fascinated with bodybuilding.

The first biceps exercise I learned—and almost the only one I did until I learned that there were other biceps exercises—was the Standing Barbell Curl. I still feel that there is no better exercise for building biceps size, as well as definition and shape, and I have always made it a part of my exercise program.

When done correctly, the Barbell Curl works basically all parts of the biceps. Note that I said "correctly." I'm a real stickler for strict exercise form. In the Curl you will only realize the full benefit of the exercise if you perform the complete movement slowly, elbows in, keeping the body straight. If you swing the weight up from your thighs to your upper chest-neck area, you will largely eliminate the biceps from the exercise. In swinging the weight you rely on the momentum of the barbell to get it up to the top position, but what you really want to do is raise the barbell with biceps strength only.

In my biceps work I've also made good use of the preacher bench. This bench was made popular by Larry Scott, who found the apparatus very effective in helping him develop his biceps to their fullest. You can use either dumbbells or a barbell in preacher-bench work, and I have used both variations with good results. But the most common mistake in using the bench, and I have seen this in gyms all across the country, is allowing the bench to be too high so that it comes right up under the armpits. What this does, of course, is cancel out the purpose of the preacher bench, which is to focus the stress on the lower part of the muscle.

I recommend keeping the preacher bench two

to three inches below the chest line. This will allow the elbows and the lower portion of the triceps to remain on the bench at all times, but not to the point where you are leaning over the bench and supporting your body weight on it. To realize the benefit of the exercise, you must stay seated and let your arms do the work; otherwise, you will not get the lower biceps roundness you're doing the exercise for in the first place.

In the movement, keep your palms out and allow the weight to go down completely so that your arms are fully extended. This seems to cause a problem for many; they curl the weight up but only let it go down part of the way. But here—just as with other exercises—extension is just as important as contraction. Also, keep your elbows slightly inward and your grip a little wider than shoulder width.

Incline Curls are beneficial in any biceps program. Each time I do them, I remember those pictures in *Muscle Builder* (now *Muscle & Fitness*) magazine of Steve Reeves doing Incline Curls. This was one of his favorite exercises, evidently, and he is largely credited with popularizing it. He would actually do the exercise until he couldn't curl the dumbbells up anymore. But rather than stopping the Incline movement, he would bring his legs into play and use them to actually kick the weights up and then resist them on the way down. A forerunner of the forced reps idea, one could say.

But unlike Steve, I think it is more productive to use strict movements. I try to use pretty heavy dumbbells, but never more than I can handle for 8–10 reps. I start with the heaviest weight I can handle correctly, then with each succeeding set I reduce it about 10 pounds. (I also use this kind of successive lowering of the weight in Preacher Curls and Standing Barbell Curls, although I lower it about 20 pounds on the latter. I usually do four sets per exercise.)

Curls on the curl machine are another part of my biceps routine and they have yielded good results. The curl machine was introduced in the late '50s or early '60s, and its development must be credited to Bob Clark, an equipment designer/manufacturer on the West Coast. The beauty of the machine is that it keeps the resistance constant throughout the movement, as opposed to the changing resistance in regular Standing Barbell Curls and Inclines, where the resistance at any point depends on the angle at which the weight is being held.

Curling the bar on the curl machine all the

"I do a form of Incline Dumbbell Curls while lying face down on the bench. You just won't believe the peak contraction you get on this exercise until you try it!"

START/"Lat Machine Pulldown Curls. . .

MIDPOINT/ . . . give me higher peak. . .

START/"Machine Curls give me biceps fullness and sweep equivalent to Preacher Curls."/MIDPOINT

. . . than any other biceps movement I've done!"/FINISH

way up to the base of the neck will give you one of the most complete movements possible for the biceps. It works the biceps throughout, even up into the shoulder where the muscle ties into the deltoids. The exercise, therefore, contracts the muscle in its strongest position, and it will help you get a very definite high crease between the biceps and the frontal deltoids.

This exercise is a favorite of mine. You can work pretty heavy on the curl machine—I use about 10 reps for four to five sets—but keep

"Barbell Curls are a biceps mainstay."

START/"Incline Curls are particularly good for the lower and outer biceps."/HALFWAY

"Narrow-grip Chins are an excellent finishing movement for biceps."

your elbows tucked in to your body and maintain control of the weight. If you can't, you're using too heavy a load.

As I change my program from time to time to keep it fresh, I like to include Lying Dumbbell Curls. These are done on an elevated bench so that you can extend the dumbbells downward without touching the floor. This full extension allows you a good stretch of the biceps and is the most important part of the movement.

I have also included palms-up, close-grip Chins in my biceps program. Look at these as curling movements in which you yourself are providing the resistance to the raising of the weight. Bring your body up to the bar as high as possible—just touching the chin to the bar is not enough. Aim to hit it, in fact, with the top part of the chest.

I have always been partial to Chins, even when I was a kid in school (I won the championship

"High-peaked biceps are an asset in any arm shot, even if it's from the back like this one."

for chinning, in fact, for my age group when I was a 13-year-old in Lake Charles, Louisiana, my hometown). I realize that some people think of them primarily as a back exercise. Well, they are excellent at developing the lats, but they work primarily and directly on the biceps, so they really should be considered an arm exercise, too.

In developing an arm routine, I take several exercises—enough to give me a good variety of movement—and group them together in the Weider "Supersets" and/or "Trisets" manner. For example, I will take the Standing Barbell Curl and group it with the Incline Dumbbell Curl and Preacher Curl. As I mentioned earlier, I use the declining weight principle in each set. Resting no more than 45 seconds between each set, I strive to do each rep as strictly as possible. This governs the weight I can use—I don't believe in cheating movements—and helps me concentrate on how the muscle is working. Then, with my biceps work done, I'm ready to move on to the big triceps muscle, which, in reality, does more than your biceps to determine the overall size of your upper arm.

How to Get Steel-Cord Forearms

by Casey Viator

Almost from the time I first became interested in bodybuilding, I've been impressed with excellent forearm development. As a result, I've consistently emphasized forearm work in my training.

Ah, forearms! That thick, corded development—almost as if bowling pins have been implanted under the skin—is a key component of every Herculean physique. If that development is missing, nothing looks as bad—particularly when the arms are hanging down at the sides.

Generally speaking, the forearms are not easy to develop. Like the calves, your forearm muscles are in constant use throughout the day. Every time you grasp an object, your forearms are moving your fingers and applying pressure to the object.

Due to the frequent daily contractions your forearm muscles must make, the muscle tissue becomes very dense and tough. And such muscle tissue is very difficult to develop. It's so tough and resistant to exercise that you have to bomb the forearms unmercifully to make any progress at all.

Very few bodybuilders have naturally large forearms. A small number of top men don't do any forearm work, and yet have tremendous forearms. Mike Mentzer does little forearm training—except for "gripping the dumbbells hard"—but his forearms are among the world's greatest.

There have never been forearms like Casey's. Here's the lowdown on how he "Weiderized" them.

In my own case, forearm development has never come easy. The rest of my body has responded extremely well, but my forearms have always been stubborn. It's only been through hard and persistent training that I've been able to build up my forearms. The hard work has been worth it, however. Some have said my forearms are now the best in the world!

As I mentioned earlier, the forearms need a tremendous amount of very intense training. When I was trying to get my forearms up a year ago, I was training them 5–6 times per week. Now that they are up, I still work them fairly hard three times a week.

My build-up routine was as follows:

Monday-Wednesday-Friday
1. Zottman Curls: 5 × 6–10 (five sets of 6–10 reps)
2. Wrist Curls: 5 × 15–20
3. Reverse Wrist Curls: 5 × 15–20

Tuesday-Thursday-Saturday
1. Reverse Curls: 5 × 6–10
2. Wrist Curls: 5 × 15–20
3. Reverse Wrist Curls: 5 × 15–20

In my biceps workouts I also do a lot of Thumbs-Up Dumbbell Curls for my brachialis muscle. This type of curl also hits the upper and outer part of my forearms. And, of course, when you use weights as heavy as the ones I use on all of my other exercises, the forearms get a pretty heavy workout just grasping the bar.

It's important for you to understand how hard I drive each set of my forearm workouts. On the Zottman Curls and Reverse Curls I go to failure on every set, and if I'm working with a training partner, I'll have him help me do some forced reps as well.

On both kinds of Wrist Curls I go to failure on the full-range reps, then do as many burns as I can handle at the end of each set. I literally work with the weight until I can't move it another inch. The barbell actually drops from my hands at times.

When I'm doing such a heavy set, I really learn the meaning of pain. But you know Joe Weider's old adage—"no pain, no gain." I just force myself through the pain zone. It hurts like the fires of hell, but I'm bolstered by the fact that there's a direct correlation between the pain and the amount of growth that results from it.

For the past few months, I've more or less been working on a maintenance program for my

START/"Reverse Curls are great for the biceps-forearm tie-in."/FINISH

forearms. This is the type of routine I now use on Mondays, Wednesdays and Fridays:

1. Reverse Curls: 4 × 6–10
2. Wrist Curls: 4 × 15–20
3. Reverse Wrist Curls: 4 × 15–20

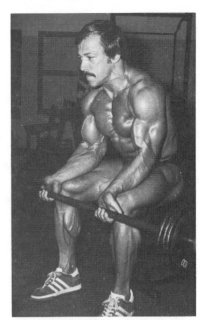

START/"Reverse Wrist Curls put steel cords in your outer forearm muscles."/FINISH

START/"I include either Zottman Curls or Thumbs-Up Dumbbell Curls in all my forearm routines."/FINISH

START/"Wrist Curls are the most basic and effective forearm movement in my routine."/FINISH

This is a pretty simple routine, and almost anyone from the intermediate level on up can use such a program effectively. If you want to accelerate your progress, you can add a set to each exercise, and up the number of workouts to 4–5 per week. And if you're a budding superstar, you can use my build-up workout.

So you don't encounter any technique problems with any of these exercises, I've described them in detail below. If you compare the exercise descriptions with the photos accompanying this article, you can't go wrong.

ZOTTMAN CURLS—This exercise is exactly like Alternate Dumbbell Curls, except that your hands must be rotated during the movement. As each hand goes up, you should supinate your hand as in a normal Alternate Dumbbell Curl. At the top rotate your thumbs inward so your hands are palms down—as in a Reverse Curl—as the dumbbell descends. Using your arms alternately and rotating your hands will be a little confusing at first, but once you master Zottman Curls,

you'll find them excellent for the upper arms and forearms.

REVERSE CURLS—This standard old exercise is superior for the upper forearms and brachialis. Take a shoulder-width reverse grip on a barbell and simply curl it up to your shoulders. For variety, you can use a narrow grip on the bar.

WRIST CURLS—Sit at the end of a bench, with your forearms against your thighs and your wrists just beyond the edge of your knees. Take a shoulder-width, palms-up grip on a barbell. Sag your fists down as low as possible and then curl the barbell up as far as you can in a half circle, keeping the forearms against your thighs. For variety, you can use a narrow grip and place your forearms along the top of a flat bench.

REVERSE WRIST CURLS—This movement is simply the opposite of Wrist Curls. Merely curl the weight with your palms down. Wrist Curls work the inner part of your forearms, while Reverse Wrist Curls exercise the outer part.

My Back-to-Basics Thigh Workout

by Dennis Tinerino

Every few days a bodybuilder with skinny legs will come up to me for advice on how to build up his thighs. How can I tell him he just isn't working hard enough?

Let's face it: nobody has ever built great legs without busting his backside at a squat rack—and nobody ever will! It takes plain, old-fashioned hard work to build big and ripped-up thighs, and a lot of bodybuilders—even at the Olympian level—seem unwilling to put in the effort.

If I were talking to the average bodybuilder with poor leg development, he'd be indignant when I told him he didn't work hard enough. "Look," he'd squawk, "I do eight sets of Sissy Squats, five sets of Leg Extensions and five sets of Lunges. Whaddaya mean I'm not working my thighs hard?!!"

I always ask, "Well, why don't you do Squats?" The answers range from "I don't want a big butt" to "my back hurts too much" or "I can get the same results with the other exercises."

All of these excuses add up to the type of stupidity that keeps a bodybuilder's legs two or three years behind his upper body in terms of development. Need I mention that it's balanced proportion that spells victory at the Olympian level?

Many of you know that I'm a big believer in basic movements. Every novice and intermediate bodybuilder should base his entire workout on one or two fundamental exercises per body part in order to build size and power. Only after

sufficient mass has been developed should one switch over to the Weider "isolation" technique of exercising to bring out the type of muscle details needed to win the big contests today.

Even the giants of the sport spend much of their time and workout energy on basic body-building movements. Most of the year they train very heavy on the basics to add mass, then switch to isolation work a few months before the Olympia to bring out more definition.

This dynamic interplay between basic and isolation exercises is the reason for the improvements I've made this year. For the first nine months after the last Olympia, I worked very hard on my weak points by doing heavy movements. I did five tons of Incline Presses per workout, 10 tons of Bent Rows and 20 tons of Deadlifts.

As I write this it's only four weeks until the Olympia, and I've been working my total body a lot harder on cables and other types of isolation work for about the last two months. I'm sure that in a few weeks this will give me the quality muscle to go with my size and improved proportions.

The basic thigh exercise is the Squat. That's not the Sissy Squat, the Hack Squat, the Front Squat, or the Bench Squat, Half Squat or Quarter Squat. It is the full Back Squat, and, yes, it is *very* hard work!

I absolutely assure you that you'll never achieve Olympian thigh development without

years of heavy squatting. A few of you will scoff at this contention, but you'll be the ones with thin thighs. I can also assure you that squatting will not give you a big butt. Mine's pretty small and I've squatted for 15 years.

When I first started bodybuilding, my legs were incredibly skinny. I think my knees were probably bigger than my thighs, so you can see that I had a long way to go. Fortunately, though, I started squatting from Day 1, and my thighs improved consistently. Eventually, they've become one of my better body parts.

At the 1979 Mr. Olympia, my thighs were a little too small, primarily because a bout of knee tendinitis had kept me from doing my usual quota of squatting. This year, however, I've hit on a solution that has allowed me to squat heavier than ever, and my thighs have really increased in size.

While working my legs, I am very careful to wrap my knees—first with neophrene rubber bands and then with elastic bandages over the rubber. The neophrene keeps in the heat, so my knees don't hurt as much when I squat. The elastic gives the joint extra stability, the same as my Weider weightlifting belt gives my abdomen and lower back additional stability when squatting.

After squatting I ice my knees, a practice I borrowed from baseball pitchers like Sandy Koufax. The icing decreases inflammation in the joint, which cuts down on pain the day after a heavy workout. It would be nice if I could forget about all of these precautions, but my knees just aren't among the best ever manufactured.

My instinctive approach to training has also taught me to squat heavy only in six-week cycles and to go down only to a position where my thighs are parallel to the floor. After six weeks of really heavy squatting (in which I handle well over 600 pounds for reps), I need a few weeks of lighter training. So I have to plan my six-week cycle to peak at contest time. Similarly, squatting past parallel is hard on my knees, so I usually place a low bench or stool in a position where my hips touch it before I go too low.

Squatting has increased the size of my thighs by 10 inches. All year long I start my thigh workouts with four or five sets of Leg Extensions to warm up my knees, and then go directly to Squats. My feet are set 16 inches apart, with my toes pointed slightly out when squatting. This works the outer sweep of my thighs, something that Bill Pearl suggested.

I start with 225 for a warm-up and then work up through five sets to the heaviest weight I can use for 4–6 reps. I've done four reps with 675 at peak strength. After I've maxed, I'll drop the weight 40–50% and do two pump sets.

When squatting heavy, it's very important to keep your torso upright and head up. Slouching and bending over at the waist with a heavy weight leaves your back open to injuries, even when you're wearing a lifting belt. And if you find that your ankles lack flexibility, you can rest your heels on a 2 × 4-inch board for better balance. I personally squat flat-footed, however.

Additional safety factors include total concentration on the exercise and a couple of spotters present during your heaviest sets to remove the weight if you're stuck. Most bodybuilders injure themselves squatting when their minds wander away from the job at hand. Total concentration is essential with the heavy weights. You also should use collars to keep plates from sliding off the ends of the bar.

On all of my exercises I try to do slow, concentrated reps. This takes full advantage of the Weider Slow Continuous Tension Principle. I

"There's no getting around it—hard work on heavy basic exercises is the only way to get championship development."—Dennis Tinerino

also like to keep my reps in the 6–8 range, which I find is best for a combination of size and cuts. On Leg Extensions I also advocate pausing at the top to utilize the Weider Peak Contraction Principle.

In the off-season I finish off my thigh workout with five sets, 6–8 reps, of Leg Curls. The major concern here is to get a peak contraction at the

"The unique angle of the hack machine throws terrific stress on the frontal thighs, as Lou Ferrigno shows here. Talk about a blowtorch burn in the quads."

"I've said it before and I'll say it again—nobody's ever built great thighs without squatting, and nobody ever will."

top and to use a complete range of motion. I really have to concentrate to keep my hips down when I do the Leg Curls. Allowing my hips to come up shortens my range of motion.

Prior to a contest I also will include four sets of Hack Squats between my Squats and Leg Curls, and I'll finish off with Lunges. I do my Hacks on the slide machine Joe Gold has built for his World Gym, where most of the top guys now train.

My final pre-contest thigh movement consists of four sets, 20 reps, of the Leg Lunge. The high reps help me to cut up my frontal thighs. If you do Lunges, be sure to emphasize stretching the thigh of the rear leg. The stretch on your rear leg is much more important than bending the front leg.

Just so there are no mistakes, here is a summary of my thigh workout:

1. Leg Extension: 4–5 × 6–8
2. Squat: 5 × 6–8 working up; 2 × 10–12 for pump
3. Hack Machine: 4 × 6–8 (pre-contest only)
4. Leg Curl: 5 × 6–8
5. Lunges: 4 × 20 (pre-contest only)

Glancing at this, you'll probably conclude that it's not a very glamorous routine. There are no fancy Sissy Squats and no exotic leg machine work. But then getting down to basics is the secret to massive, ripped-up thighs. Go for it!

Robby's Incredible Thigh Biceps

by Bill Reynolds

Robby's thigh biceps are incredible. Period.

They are, however, a little less incredible than they were a couple of years ago, which is all according to the Robby Robinson Master Plan. That plan emphasizes balance and detail in every muscle group, especially in such neglected areas as the serratus, lower back and thigh biceps. But we're getting ahead of the story. Let's start at the beginning.

"When I started training with weights I weighed about 145," Robby recalls. "I didn't have any muscle on the back of my thighs to speak of, but I was athletically inclined and I exercised all of the time. I had some pretty good upper body muscle, because I'd started exercising in grade school, and by the eighth grade, I was already trying to figure out what bodybuilding was all about. It wasn't until college, in about 1965, that I had weights to train with, but by that time I'd already been doing push-ups and chins for years.

"The first time I touched a weight I could bench press 100 pounds 10 times, which wasn't much considering the push-ups I could do, but I was totally elated just to be using weights. Since we only had 100 pounds of weights, I was soon using that poundage for everything—curls, rows, benches, triceps presses, squats.

"This shot vividly illustrates what a good thigh biceps can do for side leg width and general lower-body impressiveness!"

"A lot of my thigh biceps development can be attributed to running in high school and college (Robby has a 9.6-second 100-yard dash to his credit—*ed.*). With the weights, I was doing a lot of stiff-leg deadlifts and leg curls. I used to do one set of 25 continuous tension reps on the leg curl every day and kept at my thigh biceps until a couple of years ago when they had grown so big, they'd made my calves look small. At that point, it was necessary to make some proportion changes by working hamstrings less and calves more.

"By training them only once or twice a week, my thigh biceps aren't as big and dominant and this makes my calves look larger. Now I'm only doing one set of 50 reps per workout—25 regular reps and 25 with continuous tension. The continuous tension reps are the most important, because they are the ones that bring out the muscle and make you look bigger than you really are.

"Just as an example of how this detail can help you, I weighed 208, two weeks before the Night of the Champions last May. By the time the contest came around I was down two more pounds, but the increased muscularity made me look like I'd gained six or eight pounds! That's why I really strive for muscularity and full development now. Genetically, I have big muscles anyway, and I've developed them even bigger by years and years of training incorrectly. Now I'm on the right track, or so Joe Weider tells me.

"The thigh biceps is a very important muscle group, because it shows up in every side pose and when split up can add 25 percent to a straight back shot. A judge should see it, because everywhere he looks he wants to see some muscle. If nothing's there, he will begin to pick you apart. And if your thigh biceps isn't fully developed, your butt can look much too big.

"There is no excuse for not having good hamstrings, because there's no way you can miss working them when you do frontal thighs and lower back. One common mistake is using tons of weight on leg curls, which doesn't develop the muscle as much as the tendons attaching the muscles to the bone. You have to make the muscles *feel* the resistance with full-range movements and a slow cadence.

"I also see a lot of people at Gold's doing leg curls with their butts in the air, or with their torsos up off the bench. This shortens the range of motion considerably and robs your muscles of potential development. The right way to do leg

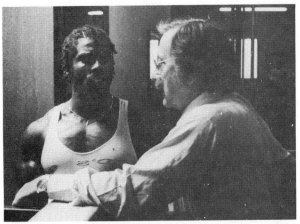

"Robby, our readers would like to know how you developed the most incredible thigh biceps in the game."

"Joe, you really take your readers seriously and give them exactly what they want. Here's precisely how I developed my thigh biceps."

curls is with your hips and torso on the bench so the leg biceps do all the work.

"Moderate weights and continuous tension are keys to developing muscle. I used to train exceptionally heavy, but with proper form and moderate poundages—plus the right mental attitude—I now gain muscle faster than I used to. The idea is to slow down each rep so you can feel it every inch of the way. Some people might do press-downs and push the bar down so fast that they miss the whole movement. There are a lot of fibers in there that aren't being stimulated that way, because momentum is doing most of the work for you. Needless to say, that's the wrong way to train.

"It's also vital to use a lot of variety when working thigh biceps, because it's a multifaceted muscle group just like the back and needs numerous movements to reach its full potential of development. My favorite exercises for thigh biceps have been stiff-leg deadlifts, floor lunges, lunges up onto a bench and leg curls. These

seem to hit every facet of my thigh biceps.

"I especially like the lunges for the stretch they give me, because stretching is one of the most important parts of my developmental program. It works the insertions and brings out maximum muscle detail. This year I've utilized more stretching movements for all body parts than last year, and I think it's working more of the muscle mass.

"For those interested in improving their thigh biceps, I'd suggest a program of leg curls, light stiff-leg deadlifts and lunges—all with continuous tension reps. Do anywhere from one to three sets of each, depending on your ability level, and do the exercises for thigh biceps after you've worked your frontal thighs. Keep your reps fairly high, say in the range of 15–20 for each set. You don't need to use super-heavy weights, but you do need to keep tension on your hamstrings throughout the movement.

"If you're after a secret exercise technique for thigh biceps, I'll give you one you've never read before. In the gym I see everyone doing leg curls with only one foot position, which doesn't give you the completeness of development you could have by using the three positions you probably do for calves. Do some sets with your toes in, some with them out, and some straight ahead. Sometimes I change my foot position twice within a set, so I can hit all three positions.

"From here, success is just a matter of psyching yourself up to push hard mentally and physically every training session. I push myself now to the point that I'm so burned out I can't swallow a drink of water for the first 30 minutes after a workout. You can feel things you never felt before if you push hard enough, and your reward will be results you never got before. Sure it hurts, but as they say, *'no pain, no gain.'*"

Lunge—START   **Lunge—FINISH**

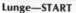

Stiff-Leg Deadlift—START   **Stiff-Leg Deadlift—FINISH**
Leg Curl—FINISH

Leg Curl—START

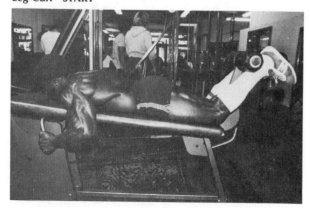
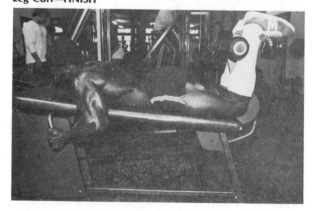

Outstanding Calves:
Bodybuilding's Diamonds—
and Just As Rare

by Mike Mentzer

"Powerful, flared calves are the base on which any great physique stands. Puny calves are to a bodybuilder what a weak foundation is to a high-rise."

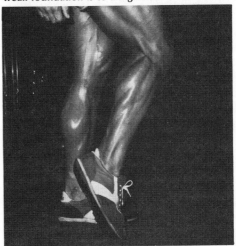

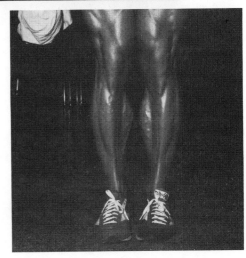

Marilyn Monroe may well have been telling the truth when she breathed, in a song of the same title, that "diamonds are a girl's best friend." Actually this line could have been lifted from the vernacular of the bodybuilder, for if diamonds are a girl's best friend, diamonds (as in diamond-shaped calves) are a bodybuilder's best friend.

When you stop to consider the dearth of fully developed, power-packed calves in the ranks of even world-class bodybuilders, you'll have to admit to the validity of the above claim. While pendulous pecs and blockbuster biceps abound in bodybuilding, a really outstanding pair of calves is still a rare commodity.

Jack Neary, in his *Muscle Builder* (now *Muscle & Fitness*) report of the 1976 American Bodybuilding Championships, quoted me referring to Roger Callard's lower legs as "full-grown cows," since they had obviously matured from being mere calves. Roger's calves, along with Ken Waller's, are among the greatest of all time, because in addition to being large and shapely, they also appear fully developed from all angles.

A head-on, frontal view of Ken Waller's calves reveals bulging inner and outer heads, as well as a thickly developed tibialis anticus. Ken's calves are perhaps most striking when he does a side pose. All of the more intricate muscles on the

lateral aspect of his lower leg, such as the peroneus brevis and longus, and the large flexor longus hallicus, lift and separate into their respective grooves while popping out at you.

Callard's calves are most spectacular when viewed from the back. When Roger strikes his famous double-biceps back pose, he clutches at the floor with his toes, causing the inner and outer heads of his gastrocnemius to divide longitudinally into two distinct muscular entities. With tendons rising and disappearing beneath mounds of flesh, and long serpentine veins zigzagging their way back and forth under the parchment-like skin that shrouds his calves, Roger looks like a modern-day Hercules.

My own calves have become something of a conversation piece in bodybuilding circles. In addition to being large (a tad shy of 19 inches cold) and bulbous, they undergo a unique metamorphosis when I flex them. Instead of just flaring on the sides and becoming more angular, as do the calves (when flexed) of most bodybuilders, the inner head of my calf breaks out into a startling amalgam of knots and knobs, like no other calf I've ever seen. This peculiar characteristic is congenital, of course, and cannot be "trained into a calf." With calves, more than any other body part, the eventual size and shape that can be attained seems to be determined genetically.

In my opinion, the logic that guides the calf workouts of most bodybuilders is fallacious. While correctly assuming that the calves are an overworked muscle, considering their integral function in walking, running and climbing, their logic breaks down when they go on to assume that this means the calves need more work (in terms of straight volume) to make them grow.

If the calves have become obstinate and refuse to grow because they are overworked from normal daily activity, don't give them more high-rep, high-set, low-intensity activity, which duplicates the effect of walking, climbing, etc. What the calves require is harder, more intense activity. Remember that intensity refers to lifting the heaviest possible weights over the fullest possible range of movement in the shortest time possible. And when you do that, not that much exercise in terms of actual amount is either possible or needed.

My present routine is as follows:

1. *Toe Press on leg machine*—Place the balls of your feet on the edge of the foot placement board on the Leg-Press machine. Allow the weight to fully extend your foot so that your heels are higher than your toes and the calves are completely stretched. I perform my first set with as much as 700 pounds for 8–12 reps, and my second set with a much lighter weight after minimal rest, again for about 8–12 reps. Both sets are performed to the maximum with as much weight as possible in as short a period as possible.

2. *Seated Calf Raises*—This exercise is either performed in conjunction with the Toe Press as part of a superset, in which case it follows the Toe Press with absolutely zero rest between the two, or it is done as a single isolated exercise following the two sets of Toe Presses. This exercise will stress the often neglected soleus, which rides under the gastrocnemius. Here again I emphasize the full stretch and go as high on my toes as I can—like a ballet dancer—when in the contracted position. The full extension and stretch at the bottom position of all calf exercises will serve to fully contract and peak the tibialis anticus, the large muscle on the front of the calf. I do two sets, 8–12 reps per set.

3. *Standing Toe Raise*—The standard Toe Raise on the calf machine is performed last in my routine. I use it to build mass and to give the calves a burn-out. I do one set of this exercise with maximum poundage, sometimes as much as 1000 pounds.

This calf routine is performed twice a week, on Mondays and Thursdays following my thigh workout. Even if nature was stingy and didn't endow you with naturally good calves, don't despair. Your calves will improve with the proper application of a high-intensity routine like the one I've just outlined.

"The seated calf machine is essential for full soleus development."

"I work calves with the same super intensity I'd use for any other bodypart."

START/"The calf machine is invaluable. . .   . . .as long as you use perfect form."/FINISH

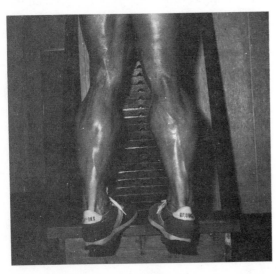

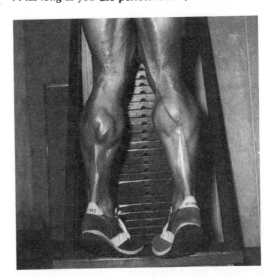

START/"I use extremely heavy weights. . .

MIDPOINT/ . . . on the leg-press machine. . .

. . .and the heavier the weight used in good form, the larger the calves!"/FINISH

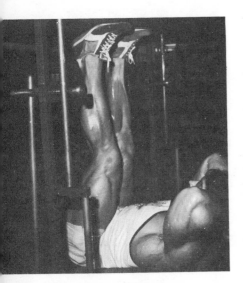

them. On the Aerosmith trail in '88, tour manager Doug Goldstein went for an early morning round of golf on the course at the band's hotel and met with the sight of Duff, Slash and Steven – each huddled in his own motorised golf cart – racing the wrong way up the fairway and looking like rock's own Banana Splits!

What next for the definitive rock 'n' roll band of the age?

"We have a lot of stuff written," says Axl. "There are probably 30 songs to choose from already. We have about 10 ballads that I feel are more credible than 'Sweet Child O' Mine'."

'November Rain', which is eight minutes long, is among them.

"We wanted to save those ballads, because we wanted to wait until we had a bigger audience. We never imagined it would be this big, but we have some songs which we've been waiting to spring on people for a long time."

One off-the-wall number that is scheduled for inclusion on the new record is the rap song which Guns N' Roses played for two weeks on the Iron Maiden tour before Axl's voice gave in.

"Other than that, we're going to try and make the longest record that we can. We're going to try and put down as many songs as we can. I don't know if it will be a very, very long single album or maybe a double album."

"Rock 'n' roll is based on attitude," asserts Slash.

"We want to tour, travel, continue the big Guns N' Roses adventure," says Axl. "And indulge ourselves. And fuck a lot! Drug use is not in the past. We scare the shit out of each other because we don't want to lose what we have as a family."

> "This band is so realistic in what we do and what we play. We never said we were the best rock 'n' roll band in the world so don't judge us as that. We just go out and play."

It's Axl who has recently held Guns N' Roses together. The pressures of a hard and fast rock 'n' roll lifestyle had begun to tell as the band played four shows at the Los Angeles Coliseum as support to the re-

animated Rolling Stones. Early reports said that Axl had wigged out, that before the show he'd driven to the backstage area at the wheel of an LAPD squad car, siren wailing. And that he'd announced from the stage that he was quitting Guns N' Roses because too many of the band were "dancing with Mr Brownstone."

The last of these rumours bears the seed of truth. Axl was desperate to shake Slash, Izzy and Steven out of drugged stupors and felt the only way he'd do it was to threaten to quit the band. It worked.

On the second night Axl told the crowd there'd be no split. Slash said his piece on the perils of narcotics. He and Izzy and Steven cleaned up. Guns N' Roses survived.

"There *is* a self-destructive element about this band," concludes Slash, "but the will to survive is infinitely stronger — about twice as strong — and that will ensure we're gonna be around for some time to come."